THE
BORDER
LINE

ERIC ROBSON

FRANCES LINCOLN LIMITED
PUBLISHERS

For Annette

Frances Lincoln Ltd
4 Torriano Mews
Torriano Avenue
London NW5 2RZ
www.franceslincoln.com

A catalogue record for this book is available from
the British Library.

ISBN 13: 978-0-7112-2716-3

Printed and bound in Great Britain by
Cox & Wyman Ltd, Reading, Berkshire

1 3 5 7 9 8 6 4 2

Maps on pages 6–8 taken from James Logan Mack, *The Border
Line: From the Solway Firth to the North Sea Along the Marches of
Scotland and England*, Oliver and Boyd, Edinburgh, 1924.

NOTE ON PLACE NAMES
Many Border place names have historically been (and sometimes
still are) spelled in a variety of ways. Where there is a choice I
have opted for the spelling most familiar to me.

CONTENTS

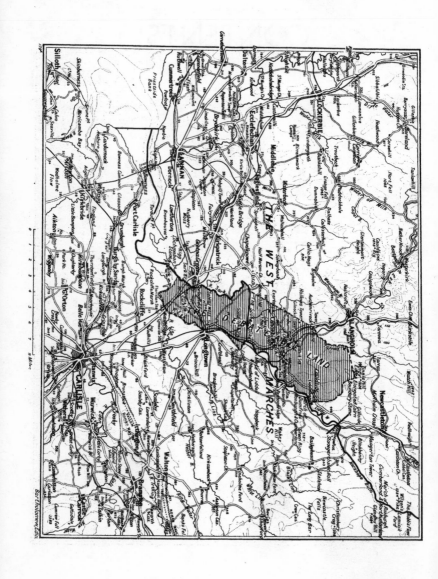

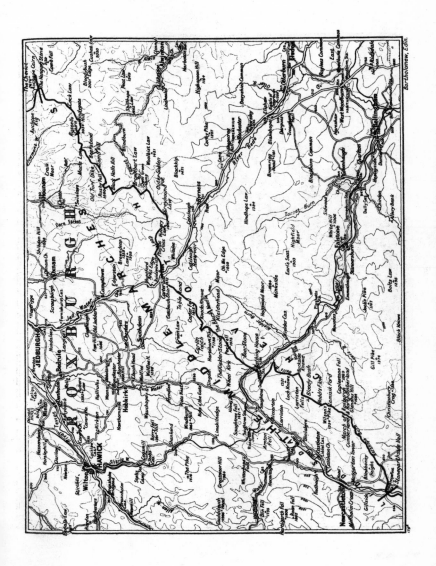

7

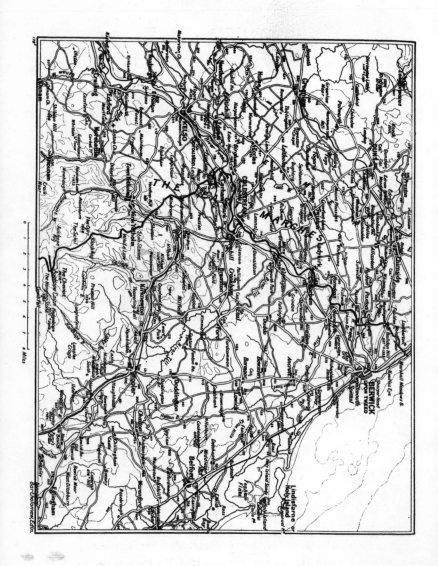

CHAPTER ONE

Above The start of the journey: the mouth of the River Sark
Pages 6-8 Maps taken from James Logan Mack, The Border Line, 1924

The River Sark is a thin streak in the mud. And the mud sucks. As I tried to pull out one wellied foot and then the other, I skited into the water. As I tried to pull out one hand and then the other, I sank in further. A shaven-headed man walking his pit bull terrier along the riverbank cheerily shouted across to ask if I was trying to commit suicide. Waving a wet sleeve, I made a joke of it. I suggested that the mouth of the Sark may be a place where you could easily lose the will to live but, no, I was just fine. He obviously thought I was barmy. And so did I.

So this is the Border.

The three steps that got me into the clutches of the mud of Sark were the first three steps of a 105-mile walk. And this wasn't a good start.

The plan was to walk the length of the Border between England and Scotland from the Solway Firth to the North Sea coast. It's a walk that hardly anybody does. Having looked out on the approach to the Promised Land from a crotch-soaked kneeling position – one wet knee in England, the other in Scotland – I could understand why. Scruffy fields are festooned with high-voltage power lines and cut through by a derelict railway embankment. And in centre frame a piddling river decorated with discarded breezeblocks and an abandoned supermarket trolley leads the eye to the bungaloid suburbs of Gretna and Springfield. It's a place in need of an inspiration transplant.

But this is supposed to be one of the most romantic and most fought-over frontiers in all of Europe. A place where two proud nations spent four centuries indulging in seriously anti-social behaviour.

I started to wring myself out and turned my back on it. And when I looked out to sea the romance and the turbulence were all there in wide screen. Cue music. The sunset tide running in along the Solway past a dead and bleached tree trapped in the sands. Angry black cloud above the distant Lakeland mountains. And wet underpants.

Start again.

I set off along the Scottish shore. Trying to take my mind off cold, wet, flapping trousers, I tried conjuring up the ghosts of history that were supposed to stalk the Border. I wondered if Shaven Head, wandering in front of me with his dog, could have been a descendant of one of the marauding Scots that the old gossip Camden wrote about in 1586: 'A warlike kind of men who have been infamous for robberies and depredations. For they dwell upon Solway Frith, a foordable arm of the sea at low waters through which they made many times out-rodes into England for to fetch in Booties.'

But our man showed no sign of depredating. In fact he unravelled the illusion completely by giving his dog a hug when it was clever enough to bring back its ball. He was probably on his way to buy bootees at Mothercare. So much for the enduring power of the genes.

Then I spotted it. In the middle of a field. An eight-foot-high chunk of rock that had the self-assurance of something much bigger. A stone with attitude. A boulder that had lived a bit since the days when it had been part of a circle of sacred monoliths. I'd come to the Lochmabonstone.

Since time unremembered this was the spot where tribal leaders would gather. After them came Scots raiding parties. Johnstones, Bells, Irvines and Armstrongs, depending on which of them weren't feuding with each other at the time, would meet here on moonlit nights before plunging across one of the treacherous Solway fords to rob and burn in Wigton and Penrith and Appleby. An even more impressive sight would have been them driving their herds of stolen cattle back across the sands ahead of the running tide.

Later, poachers turned gamekeepers like the Maxwells and Musgraves would meet here to hold court as Lord Wardens of the West March, one of the three administrative divisions of the Border. Here they'd act out the stately and sometimes bloody rituals of the Border law and pretend that everything was normal. As powerful and unscrupulous men do now on the borders of Bosnia or Chechnya and along the warlord frontier between Afghanistan and Pakistan.

As the sun started its descent behind the Isle of Man, the Lochmabonstone cast a long shadow. The two bands of horsemen turned away. The English made a dash to beat the Solway tide. The Scots faded into the gloaming. Maybe the walk would be worth doing after all.

I was doing it for 'Simmon'. That's how he was universally known the length of the Waverley line – the North British Railway Company route from Carlisle to Edinburgh which was closed in the 1960s in an act of political vandalism justified, as they so often are, by sleight-of-hand economics.

Simon Bell was my grandfather and his influence on me was out of all proportion to the five years I knew him before he died. I was a little boy who loved trains and for a time Simon had the distinction of being the only stationmaster with platforms in both England and Scotland. He ran Kershopefoot and Newcastleton stations. Not that he needed additional distinction. He was one of those naturally talented men who rose beyond poverty and rudimentary education to become wise and respected. He was a JP; he sorted out intractable village disputes; he wrote letters on subjects of terrible delicacy for those who couldn't write; he was the voice of the village when authority in its various states of fancy dress bore down too heavily. Even though he'd been born across the Border in north Cumberland, he knew his adopted corner of the Scottish Borders better than people who'd been there all their lives.

So it was that on a frostbitten day in the 1920s one James Logan Mack was making his way along the up platform of Newcastleton station to visit Simmon. (And in that statement is our first clue about the pecking order of the two proud nations that face each other across this Border. The up platform was the one from which trains went south to London. It was down to Edinburgh, whatever the map may suggest to the contrary.) Anyhow, Logan Mack was a fifth-generation Edinburgh lawyer fifty-odd years old and with a taste for exploration. He'd already been through the Canadian Rockies and the West Indies, Morocco and Iceland and Spitzbergen.

His latest adventure was to walk the Border line. He was going to see how much physical evidence of it remained on the ground. It would take six summers of tramping from Solway to Tweed with a group of friends wearing plus fours, cowpat caps and shooters' tweeds. That day in Newcastleton he sat by the roaring fire in the stationmaster's office and drank strong tea. Between trains, Simon talked him through the lie of the land from Gretna to Kielder. He put him in touch with the local farmers. He told him stories of the Scots Dike and the Bloody Bush.

Many years later Simon told his grandson about the meeting. Many years after that I managed to buy a copy of the book that Logan Mack wrote to record his exploration of the frontier – *The Border Line*, released by the Edinburgh publishers Oliver and Boyd in 1924. A second edition followed in 1926. And then there was the silence of the second-hand bookshelves.

It's a substantial, proper sort of book, three hundred and more pages, dark blue embossed with gold lettering. There's a dedication on the flyleaf of my copy: 'Marjorie Robson-Scott from her mother. 18th March 1925'. Knowing that the Robsons and the Scotts had been on opposite sides for most of the centuries of Border turmoil, for them to be on such hyphenated speaking terms seemed a hopeful sign of progress. The frontispiece photograph is of the author, a sombre man dressed in tweeds and spats standing at the Hanging Stone on Cheviot. With narrowed eyes he's looking south to far horizons. He would have been hard pressed to look either east or west, so fearsomely starched is his gleaming collar.

The Border Line is a classic work of amateur scholarship. Detailed and a bit pompous. But I imagine you wouldn't expect a lot of laughs from a fifth-generation Edinburgh lawyer, who was remembered by his friends as a meticulous planner who organized his explorations with forensic efficiency. His book has detailed descriptions of every nut, bolt and fencepost but little sense of the excitement of the exploration, the thrill of the chase. In all its 316 pages Logan Mack hardly ever expresses frustration or delight. But for three-quarters of a century *The Border Line* was the definitive book on the subject. No detailed account of the frontier has been written since. A broadcasting colleague of mine, Bob Langley, wrote a book about his walk along the Border in the 1970s. From it I learned many interesting things such as how to keep a campfire smouldering overnight under a square of turf. This would be of little practical use to me, as I had not the slightest intention of camping with the Kielder midges.

Then in 2003 the writer Alistair Moffat asked me if I'd like to join him for a stroll along the Border for a television series commissioned by ITV called *Walking the Line*. It was four weeks of argumentative good fun. Grumpy old men on tour. Most of this walk was done by car and helicopter.

I told myself that what I really needed to do was get to the interesting bits of the Border without benefit of paraffin budgie. Which is why you find me dozing against the Lochmabonstone listening to the seabirds and imagining the clatter of departing hoofs.

CHAPTER TWO

The famous Blacksmith's 'Marriage shop' at Gretna Green

The geographic departure point is easy, the historic more troublesome.

According to the Ordnance Survey, the Border line in the west starts in the middle of the Solway low-water channel, close to the hamlet of Newbie near Annan. It then runs with the tide to the confluence of Eden and Esk before disappearing like a rat up a drain along the River Sark.

Historically there are any number of starting points. We could go back to AD 120 and Hadrian's Wall, the first example of any sort of frontier in these parts running roughly from west to east. Earlier tribal boundaries had tended to run north–south. But Hadrian's Wall was built more as a political statement than a border between rival nations. It was the Emperor's line in the sand. Thus far and no further. Rome's policy of continual expansion was no longer manageable or affordable. It would no longer be an empire without end. Yes, the wall had a frontier function. It was probably whitewashed on its northern face to make it seem more impregnable than it really was. It had customs checkpoints and defensive fortifications to prevent incursions from the north and also attacks from the south because the natives on both sides of the wall were from very similar Celtic tribes.

We could pick AD 844, when Kenneth MacAlpin united the Picts and Scots and claimed a southern border on the River Tweed.

1018 is a possibility. In that year at the battle of Carham the Scottish king Malcolm II and his sidekick, Owain the Bald, ruler of the kingdom of Strathclyde, annihilated the English. (Was he really called Owain the Bald to his face? Was being follically challenged a status symbol in 1018? These are the sort of things that proper historians ought to tell us.)

Anyhow, the battle was scarcely worth the fighting. The result was a foregone conclusion. A comet had appeared for thirty nights before the action, foretelling the victory and confirming the eastern section of the Border line on the River Tweed. But the same year in the west there must have been a shortage of predictory comets. The muddle continued. The ancient Welsh kingdom of Cumbria was amalgamated with the Gaelic kingdom of Scotia. Such rulers as existed in the borderlands looked north to Dunfermline to find their overlord rather than south to London or Winchester. The western part of the notional boundary called the Border line would have been somewhere about Morecambe Bay.

Skip across seventy-four years and you find William Rufus building his castle at Carlisle and taking Cumberland back for the Norman English.

> King William went . . . to Carlisle and restored the city and erected the castle and drove out Dolfin [son of Cospatric, the Earl of Northumbria] who had ruled the country and garrisoned the castle with his men and then came south and sent many peasant people back there with their wives and cattle to live there and cultivate the land.[1]

This enforced settlement of Cumberland was a powerful demonstration of William's determination to keep what he'd conquered and there's no bolder expression of finality on the whole Border than Carlisle Castle. But not even this clenched fist of sandstone could sort it.

During the anarchy of King Stephen's reign, less than half a century later, David I of Scotland reoccupied Carlisle and struck even further south. In the west everything north of the River Ribble was controlled by Scotland and Stephen was bullied into giving most of the earldom of Northumberland to

---

1 *Anglo-Saxon Chronicle*, Everyman Press, 1912

the Scots. He did have one moment of glory, though. In 1149 Stephen arrived unexpectedly at York with an army big enough to face down David's Scottish forces. Had he not, the Scots grip on the north would have been complete. David I would have ruled from his twin capitals of York and Edinburgh and the country we know as England would have been confined to the midlands and the south.

When David died in 1153 (in Carlisle as it happens, where the King lay among his household, his archives and his treasure) the Scots throne passed to his twelve-year-old son, Malcolm IV. Four years later Malcolm was persuaded to give up his claims to Northumberland and Cumberland to his cousin Henry II. And so far we've only got to the middle of the twelfth century.

Midsummer's day 1314 could be a contender. The day the forces of Robert the Bruce routed the English army of Edward II at Bannockburn. A victory that, six years later, led to the Declaration of Arbroath, which affirmed Scottish independence.

Unsurprisingly, Arbroath is better known for its smokies: Declaration or no Declaration, a great deal of blood would flow under the bridge before Scotland got the freedom it wanted.

There were to be almost four hundred years of border squabbles and incursions before the Act of Union in 1707 supposedly settled things once and for all. It didn't. On a map published as late as 1837 some bits of the line were still marked as disputed ground. Even if the remaining problems were sorted out shortly afterwards (which they probably weren't) it had taken about 1,720 years to fix the Border line. And that's a frontier dispute of Balkan proportions.

So now is as good a time to start as any. If the Border's running true to form we'll find there's still disputed territory along the way. The journey will take me from the flat lands of the Solway Plain with its panoramic skies through the biggest planned forest in Europe. Beyond that there will be more than forty miles of high-level walking along the Cheviot watershed before the drop to the River Tweed and a meander to the North Sea coast.

For much of the way the Border follows natural features – rivers, streams and watersheds – but it's still not natural. It's there because somebody put it there, and because it's manmade it's temporary. All borders are. Just compare a school atlas of the 1920s with the up-to-the-minute version to see how impermanent once-important strategic frontiers can be. But our Border is an oddity among borders. By rights it should have faded from the maps following the Union of the English and Scots Parliaments in 1707. But it didn't. Instead it lingered on as an emotional rather than a geopolitical frontier. We might have had to reinvent it with the creation of the new Scottish Parliament in 1999, but if it hadn't already been there would we have bothered?

(Of course, anyone of Scottish Nationalist persuasion would take a rather different view. Proud, independent Scottish Nation and all that. But talk of full-blown independence for a tiny, underpopulated bit of offshore Europe seems to me to be straying dangerously close to Prisoner of Zenda territory with Jimmy Logan rather than Ronald Coleman playing the lead. But I wouldn't like you to get the impression I've any strong view about these things.)

Seems to me that we're going to be walking along what in many ways is an imaginary line. Just as the theatre director Ronald Eyre discovered when he was asked to explore the border between Ulster and the Irish Republic for a BBC Television series. 'All the time I was doggedly pursuing a geographical line called the Irish Border, I had to learn that the real border is between two religions, histories, sets of perceptions and is carried in the bloodstream and the head.'[2]

The Border from Solway to Tweed, too, was always an artificial, arbitrary division cutting through the middle of an area with a deep-rooted cultural and political independence. As the historian W.M. Aird wrote in his crisp *Northern England or Southern Scotland*, 'This regional identity made the Anglo-Scottish frontier permeable to the extent that it was almost negligible.'[3]

But before I talk myself out of doing this walk by convincing myself the line isn't really there, I think perhaps we'd better break for the Border.

I began my extensive preparations for the trip at 8.20 a.m., kissed the dog, patted the children and told my wife, Annette, that I might be some time. I left at half past. I'm a spur-of-the-moment traveller. I could say I travel light but anyone who's seen my fifteen-stone silhouette on a hill would probably quibble. Spare pair of socks and underpants, toothbrush and toothpaste is all you need. And maps and a compass for the high-level bit across the Cheviots. Despite my naturally lethargic pace I often pass walkers equipped as if for world circumnavigation. They trudge under an overhang of rucksack that, at the very least, must contain the contents of an aisle at Sainsbury's. Perhaps they have peculiar dietary requirements. Perhaps they dress for dinner. Perhaps they can't sleep away from home without a pot hot-water bottle. Perhaps it's gin. Whatever it is, they should seek help.

'But what happens if we get soaked?' I hear you grumble, even at this early stage beginning to doubt the wisdom of venturing anywhere with this sloppily ill-prepared walking companion.

2 Ronald Eyre et al, *Frontiers*, BBC Books, 1990
3 W.M. Aird, *Northern England or Southern Scotland*, Sutton, 1997

You stand in front of a pub fire and dry out, of course. And what are hotel radiators for if not to dry your underpants overnight? (And if there's a sign that says 'Don't cover the radiator', well, don't cover the bloody radiator. Put your underpants on the towel-warming rail instead.)

'And what happens if we get lost?'

Keep walking downhill (carefully) and you'll eventually come to somewhere. This is a very small and crowded island and you're unlikely to fall off the edge into the sea. If you do find yourself falling into the sea, you're very lost and your family should arrange to have locks put on your bedroom door immediately.

'And what happens if we break a leg?'

I can assure you that nothing you can carry in your rucksack will be the slightest use. Even the most basic Mobile Army Surgical Hospital requires quite a large lorry.

And if you're struck by lightning, you'll be dead.

So, assuming you haven't been, let's get on with it.

I'm certainly not going to be purist about this exploration of the Border. This walk is unashamedly based on personal whim. What gets in is what takes my fancy. Stories that spring from the map. So, to start as we mean to go on, the first ten miles up the Solway can go hang. Walking on water has never been my strong suit, as the aforementioned experience at the mouth of the Sark confirms. And so on a brightish morning, with ominous cloudbanks creeping in behind me from the Irish Sea, I set off up the river. First on the English side and then, at a little weir of what looks like builders' rubble, across to the Scots.

Along the way I'm going to be looking for clues about how important the Border line is today. I've always described myself as a Borderer, but what bits of 'Borderness' do I share with people along the way? Does this leaky frontier mark out differences of character, differences in attitude? Do the people who live around it have more in common with each other than with the arms-length English of Manchester or the far-flung Scots of Motherwell? Why have the families whose names constantly appeared on the charge sheet of Border history stayed rooted to the place in a way that hasn't happened elsewhere in the British Isles, except perhaps in the Scottish Highlands and Cornwall? Has the creation of a largely autonomous Scottish Parliament given the Border a greater significance?

Which are quite enough questions to be going on with.

But this isn't a single-issue walk. A plate of tatties alone is a dreary thing. So I'm going to be adding the gravy of digression and detour when the fancy takes me.

As now, as I try to keep your interest (and mine) while negotiating the dreary dribble of Sark.

The abandoned railway is a clue. We're walking through what was once the most secret place in Britain and the biggest munitions factory ever built. Nine miles long, it stretched from Eastriggs along the Scottish Solway coast and across the Sark to Longtown in England, where the Ministry of Defence still runs a munitions depot. It was known simply as H.M. Factory. Behind its security fences 30,000 workers, most of them women, kneaded nitroglycerine and nitro-cotton into an explosive paste called cordite. When the author Conan Doyle visited the factory he memorably described the paste as the Devil's porridge. In 1915 British troops in France had been running short of ammunition. H.M. Factory, built here on the west coast in an attempt to keep it safe from German Zeppelin attack, would ensure a constant supply. Garden city townships were built at Eastriggs and Gretna to house the workforce, but officially these places didn't exist. They were known only by their codename – Moorside.

But the navvies who built the factory and the workers who laboured there turned this corner of the border into another battlefield. Having drunk Moorside dry, they would move on to Annan and then across the Border to Longtown and Carlisle. Commentators of the time described the scenes of drunken debauchery as resembling a Hogarth cartoon. So in 1916 Lloyd George's government introduced the Defence of the Realm Act – known, not altogether affectionately, as DORA. Among its provisions was state control of the drinks trade. Pubs and breweries were nationalized in a swathe of country around the Factory and into England as far as Carlisle and Maryport. (Similar schemes were introduced around naval installations on the Cromarty Firth and in buffer zones around the gun factory at Enfield in Middlesex.)

New rules were imposed – spiritless Saturdays, no treating (in effect a prohibition on buying anyone else a drink), a ban on heaters and coolers which meant you couldn't drink beer and spirits in the same pub. You weren't allowed to stand at a bar and government inspectors lurked under streetlamps to check that the new salaried pub landlords were practising 'disinterested management' – that they weren't allowing people to get drunk in their government-owned pubs. From the start it was described as an experiment. It was still being described as such in the early 1970s when the Conservative Home Secretary Willie Whitelaw, MP for Penrith and the Border, sold it off. To this day nobody's sure if the experiment worked, but it's widely credited with keeping the marauding Temperance Leagues at bay and Britain from the Prohibition madness that swept America.

I head for Moorside and a drink. It owns up to being Gretna on the road signs these days. I find I can buy both spirits and beer, that I can stand to drink and treat whomsoever I like (but I choose not to) and that the nearest I can find to disinterested management is the girl behind the bar who's more concerned with checking the integrity of her fingernails than giving the right change to people who have the audacity to be customers. Maybe she was called Dora.

Gretna and its more famous neighbour Gretna Green are not what you could call picturesque. The centre of Gretna reminds me of a run-down military base in some abandoned imperial outpost where the locals exercised squatters' rights after the army moved out. Gretna Green is leafier, but the row of derelict shops and hotels dominating its main street rather takes the edge off what few charms it has.

It was an English Act of Parliament that made Gretna Green one of the most famous villages in Scotland. Lord Hardwicke's Marriage Act of 1754 made marriages conducted anywhere other than in church illegal in England; moreover, no one under the age of twenty-one could be married without their parents' permission. Essentially it was an attempt to stop wealthy young heiresses being spirited off by unscrupulous fortune-hunters. Maybe because fortune-hunters north of the Border tended to be shot, Scotland saw no need to change its marriage laws. The age of consent without parental approval stayed at sixteen. Handfasting, where a couple simply had to declare a wish to marry in front of witnesses, was legal in Scotland up to 1940.

Gretna Green was the first village in Scotland on the old coaching road to the north. Runaway couples, often with angry parents in hot pursuit, would dash over the border and into the blacksmith's shop for a quick hitching. It was a lucrative business. One self-styled 'minister' reckoned he'd married more than three thousand couples in the twenty-nine years he'd been doing the job. Men like the blacksmith priest Joseph Paisley whose day jobs were fishing and smuggling would charge £50 or even £100 a time for an instant wedding over the anvil. 'As hammer and anvil join metal together in the heat of the fire, I hereby join this couple together in the heat of the moment. Fifty quid please.' Nice work if you could get it. But chicken feed compared to what the place is earning today as the most successful privately owned tourist attraction in Scotland. Only Edinburgh Castle gets more visitors. Hundreds of couples still get married here every year even though they aren't running away from anything. (Anything on horseback or in a carriage and pair at any rate.)

Most days you can find hopefuls in all shapes and sizes acting out the history of the place, driven to the marriage room by liveried coachmen. Nowadays they're welcomed by a piper in full highland rig and married by one of a rota of church ministers who've sent so many couples from Gretna Green to Elysium that, try as they might, you can't help feeling they're on autopilot. And between the real weddings there are mock marriages to entertain the coach parties. They're proof, if indeed proof were needed, that the British on holiday suspend all judgement and will laugh at anything.

The flight to Gretna touched a voyeuristic streak in the English. The newspapers began to carry stories that nudged and winked at their readers. 'On Wednesday se'night set out for the Temple of Hymen Mr. Cuttle, jnr. Of Hatheroyd near Barnsley, with Miss E. Dickens of Knottingley; a young lady about 16 with a fortune of £3,000.'[4]

Gretna Green had become risqué and romantic. Its tourist popularity turned it into the most Scottishy place in Scotland even though it's less than a mile from the border as the runaway bride flies. Attached to the tiny smiddy these days is an out-of-town shopping mall of Wal-Mart proportions. Fed by a steady stream of coach parties, it overflows with tartans

4 *Leeds Intelligencer*, 16 November 1799

and knick-knacks dedicated to what some marketing man has decided is the essence of Scottishness. Accordion music and fluffy Loch Ness monsters, shortbread and computer-printable clan histories. You can even buy a Scottish passport.

I wandered round with a couple of Japanese tourists who seemed to think they were in Edinburgh. I told them they were in hell. But they still bought a very Scottish fridge magnet.

It's a mystery to me. Why is it, do you suppose, that tartan tattery seems to transcend national and cultural boundaries with such ease? The Italians and the Americans are as keen to buy it as the Japanese. Even the greatest cultural snobs of the lot, the French, buy it. Is it because it's immediately distinctive? Kitsch with a sense of place. And for all its faults at least Scotland is bold enough and self-confident enough to proclaim an identity. Travel north across the Border and at places like Gretna Green Scotland is immediately in your face. Travel south and what do you get? Southwaite motorway services on the M6, where the only distinctive Englishness is to be found sweating and curling under the heat lamps of the cafeteria counter. Only the English would put up with it.

Having escaped from Gretna Green, I found that even the River Sark was looking quite romantic, despite Logan Mack's dismissal of it as a sluggish, unattractive stream that wasn't worth further consideration. It was a walk through dappled shade in the band of trees that hug the riverbank. Until the weather caught up with me. Two big drops. Then ten. Then run for cover. I was sheltering beneath an ash tree straining under the weight of the rain and looking out through a waterfall when it occurred to me that this little stream marking the Border was once a blessed haunt of a particular hero of mine. During the First World War the Reverend George Bramwell Evens came to the banks of the Sark as a missionary to the navvies at the Factory. He was the Methodist minister in Carlisle. He built a prefab church and social centre in the munitions area where he tried to tempt a troublesome congregation away from the evils of the drink.

And Bram Evens knew a thing or two about addiction. He was addicted to the fishing. His daughter once told me that during a service at the Methodist Central Hall (appropriately enough in Carlisle's Fisher Street) an angling pal of his showed up at some point in mid-sermon and mimed from the door that the salmon were running in the River Eden. Three minutes later the service was over and a rather baffled congregation was left trying to work out what the minister's heavily edited message had meant, as he climbed into his waders in the vestry.

Bramwell Evens became a household name and that name was Romany of the BBC. He was the first great natural history broadcaster. His programmes on the Home Service attracted audiences of seven or eight million. With his spaniel Raq and two little girls, Muriel and Doris, played by ladies of indeterminate years, he made forays into the countryside finding birds and badgers, fish in the streams and flowers in the hedgerows. And all in a studio in Manchester equipped with a collection of sound effects discs. But he'd gathered his knowledge of the natural world in the landscapes of the English and Scottish Borders and the programmes he wove from the experience of his visits with gypsy caravan to the Eden Valley and Kershope and Penton inspired little boys like David Attenborough and David Bellamy. When he died in the 1940s, many schools in the north of England were closed as a mark of respect. Several hundred people wrote offering Raq a home. And that's a lesson I learned from Romany. The dog that walks with me on many a television programme is also called Raq – even though he's a scruffy and notoriously cantankerous border terrier – and he always gets more fan mail than the bearded chap on the other end of the string. But I wouldn't want you to think that any bitterness attaches itself to that remark.

The rain eased and the band of black cloud sauntered away to the east as I headed upriver. I was in a corridor of trees snaking through a flat, farmed landscape. But even in the confines of this narrow countryside walking is a liberation. Just in case that hint of worthiness sets alarm bells ringing, a suspicion rising that I might be in danger of taking this relatively harmless activity altogether too seriously, and as you're going to be looking over my shoulder for a hundred and more miles of it, I suppose you'd better have an idea of the sort of walker you've picked out of the bundle. I'm actually a stroller rather than a walker. I expend as little energy as possible. I don't feel guilty about not breaking sweat. If you're looking for a thundering pace and heavy breathing, I suggest you pick the next bloke on the bookshelf. Ambling and traipsing are rather more my style. Taking time to let the landscape breathe and the history to rise from the map. I'm overtaken a lot, generally by people focused on their toe ends or some vanishing point on the horizon who might as well be on a walking machine in the gym.

Now I may be slow, but at least I generally have a vague idea of where I am. It's really quite amazing how many ostensibly well-equipped walkers you come across who are utterly lost. There are telltale signs. Three people trying to read the same map while another sulks. The map turned round and round in the hope that putting north at the bottom will somehow make everything clear. And this in one of the best-mapped landscapes anywhere in the world.

'Can I help?'

'No, we're fine. Just checking our bearings.'

'Great day, isn't it? Perfect temperature for comfortable walking.'

'Yes. Eh, we're heading for somewhere called Rockcliffe.' A veiled appeal for help, which generally comes from the woman in the party.

'Well, you're just a little adrift.' It's very bad form to tell lost walkers that they're lost and going in precisely the opposite direction from the one they thought they were taking. 'I reckon you're about four inches off the side of that map.'

'See, told you,' mutters the sulker.

'Easy mistake to make.' (Apart from the tiny clue that rivers tend to flow downhill.) I walk on and leave them to their grumbling recriminations.

A love of maps is one of the things that the old fellwalker Alfred Wainwright gave me when I was filming television series with him in the 1980s. Maps as novels. The plot is the sweep of geology and history. The characters landscape features and place names that hint at a mystery or spark a memory.

And there was the name. Quintinshill. Printed just a couple of fields away on the other side of the Sark. It was a name that could bring a tear to Simmon's eye. The scene of Britain's worst-ever railway disaster. At 6.49 a.m. on 22 May 1915 a troop train carrying almost five hundred officers and men of the Royal Scots on their way to Gallipoli ran into a stationary goods train at Quintinshill. Less than a minute later a northbound express ploughed into the wreckage. The troop train was telescoped to a third of its length. Its gaslit wooden carriages caught fire. The roll-call of casualties was 227 dead and 246 injured. Some of the trapped soldiers amputated their own arms and legs to escape from the fire. The sound of rifle ammunition exploding in the heat gave rise to a local story that officers had shot their injured men.

Above me in a tree by the River Sark a blackbird was singing after the rain. The same sound a survivor of the crash said he remembered most clearly from that May morning in 1915.

CHAPTER THREE

Debateable Land: the Border line of the Scots Dike

B efore this walk becomes more digression than progression, we'd better push on. But slowly, of course. Look for the heap of abandoned fence wire and rusting scrap pushed into the corner of a field and that's where the Border leaves the River Sark.

Now you're thinking, 'But what if the fence wire and scrap have been tidied away? How will we know which way to go if that happens?' I know you are and you mustn't worry. Heaps of rusting fence wire are there for the duration, until oxidization rather than organization removes them, and that can take thirty or forty years. And if it's any comfort, I remember a pal of mine who used to run a cross-Border taxi service in this area once asking for directions to a particularly remote farm. 'Go three miles past Easton and turn left at a red barn. Two miles more and right at a big oak tree that's fallen down on a corner. Half a mile and turn left when you see a man pushing a barrowload of lime and you'll be there,' came the reply. Barn, fallen oak and man with barrow were all in their appointed places and the farm was found. It's like that in the Borders.

We're climbing up beside a boundary line of ancient and gnarled hawthorns. In the next field is a sagging collection of agricultural buildings that would make the perfect film location for *Cold Comfort Farm*. This is the Debateable Land and ahead of us is the long, narrow plantation, stark in the flat landscape, which marks the Border line of the Scots Dike. The first mention of these lands being a matter of debate came in 1450 when, as part of a truce between the two countries, the ambassadors of Scotland undertook to read out a proclamation on the Border demanding that all claimants to the lands called 'batable' or 'threpe' in the West Marches should behave themselves and stop causing bother.

The Debateable Land isn't very big – no more than ten miles from north to south and four across, bounded by the River Sark in the west, the Liddel and the Esk in the east. But its part in the bloody history of the western border is out of all proportion to its size. It was a ghetto and a refuge, an administrative no-man's-land where the rule of law didn't run. It was the equivalent of the Wild West's Hole in the Wall, a haven for outlaws, broken men and, lowest of the low, 'clanless loons', who were the butt of everybody's ill humour. In the middle of the sixteenth century the Debateable Land would have been home to twenty times as many people as there are today. It was so overcrowded that it couldn't grow enough crops or rear enough livestock to feed its population. So what they needed they stole from the countryside round about. Steal or starve. The Debateable Land became a self-fulfilling prophecy and a place that gave the lie to the accepted wisdom that English robbed Scots and Scots robbed English. The residents of the Debateable Land claimed allegiance to England and allegiance to Scotland as it suited them. Their loyalty was portable and they rendered it to both or to neither as the situation suited. Put beyond the pale by both countries, they plundered indiscriminately and wherever they could find the easiest mark. They wouldn't be happy to rob their granny, but the granny across the hill was an altogether different matter.

The Border records are littered with references to the destabilizing effect of the Debateable Land. On 4 August 1528 William, Lord Dacre was writing to Wolsey and complaining of 'cruell murdour and shamfull slaughter' done to his servants there.

The English and Scots authorities were at their wits' end and in the middle of the sixteenth century resolved to sort things out once and for all. Their plan was that the whole of the Debateable Land would be forcibly evacuated and laid waste. Until it occurred to them that they couldn't keep it that way without permanently deploying the sixteenth-century equivalent of a UN peacekeeping force. Fearful of what, today, we would call 'mission creep', they decided instead to partition the area. And to soften up the locals in preparation for that, the Lord Wardens of both countries – the Crown officers responsible for Border security – issued a joint proclamation in 1551. Logan Mack translated this chilling official document in *The Border Line*.

> All Englishmen and Scottishmen, after this proclamation made, are and shall be free to rob, burn, spoil, slay, murder and destroy all and every such persons, their bodies, buildings, goods and cattle as do remain or shall inhabit upon any part of the said Debateable Land, without any redress to be made for the same.

In other words, if the rule of law didn't work they hoped state-sponsored anarchy would.

Stretching away through the narrow strip of woodland the Scots Dike is a forgotten monument. If it had been built by the Romans it would have a car park, interpretation centre and café. Instead it's unmarked and overgrown with trees and briars. You can just make out the remains of the pair of ditches flanking an earth embankment, once eight feet high but now a hummock in the woods. I suppose it could be worse. Without the tree cover the Scots Dike would, like as not, have been ploughed up. But as the trees fall their roots tear up the most contentious length of frontier in Britain and one of the most substantial man-made sections of the whole Border line. In places it's disappeared altogether. After Logan Mack had been here in the 1920s he wrote to the papers about the neglect of the Scots Dike and hoped that something would be done to save it. We're still waiting. When I visited the place with Alistair Moffat we stumbled across one of the sixteenth-century boundary marker stones that, at one time, had been set along the top of the Dike. It was still in one piece, buried in the leafmould. But where should we report it – to the English or the Scottish authorities? Because it was lying on the English side I decided to try English Heritage rather than Historic Scotland. Having been passed around their offices in Carlisle and Manchester and Newcastle, I gave up. The lack of interest was deafening.

But on this spot in September 1552 Wardens representing each of the powers gathered. Lord Wharton and Sir Thomas Challoner for England. Richard Maitland of Lethington and Sir James Douglas of Drumlanrig representing the Scottish Crown. The Scots Commissioners argued for a boundary line that was too far south for the English to stomach. The English Commissioners wanted a line a mile or more to the north. Fortunately the French Ambassador had been brought along as arbitrator and he diplomatically set the Border halfway between the rival claims. A straight line running due east from Sark to Esk. Unfortunately, when the workmen got round to digging the dyke they obviously started from either end. Where they met in the middle they missed by twenty-one feet. Perhaps they should have brought a French construction gang too.

The Dike itself was just one of a number of what politicians today would call 'initiatives' but which, then as now, translated as desperate measures. Marriage between English and Scots Borderers was prohibited, no Borderer could pass from his own country to the other without a safe conduct and no Scots Borderer was allowed to spend a night in Carlisle. Issuing the edict was easy. Finding a drinking dive in Carlisle's Rickergate that wasn't awash with overnighting Scots was more difficult.

At its eastern end the Scots Dike ends 'opposite the house of Fergus Greme; a cross pattee at each end and styled "this is the last and fynal lyne of the particion concluded xxiiij Septembris 1552'".

This is the first time we've fallen among Grahams on this trip. So as we fight our way through the undergrowth along the line of the Scots Dike into Graham territory, it's worth mentioning just what a troublesome bunch they were. At the time of the partition of the Debateable Land they had thirteen fortified towers in the area and it's said could put five hundred men in the saddle at the drop of a hint. They were a Scots family descended from the Caithness earls of Stratherne, but during the reign of Henry IV they were allowed to settle in England on condition that they would defend English interests. It didn't quite work out like that. They regularly turned up on the Scots side if the price was right. As a result they were loathed by the English authorities. James VI and I issued a proclamation in December 1603 which attempted to explain why he hadn't sorted out the notorious Grahams. His excuse was that he didn't have the necessary brass: 'for lack of means to provide presently for the transportation of these Grames elsewhere, to the intent their lands may be inhabited by others of good honest convictions.'

By 1606 the means had been found. King James taxed the counties of Cumberland and Westmorland to pay for the transportation of three shiploads of 'rascalties'[5] through the port of Workington to Ulster and the Low Countries. They were ordered never to return on pain of death. Government officials in Ireland complained that they were as difficult to manage in Ireland as they had been in north Cumberland. To this day in the Northern Ireland telephone directory you can

5 Palmer, *The Verge of Scotland*, Robert Hale, 1939

still find the strange name Maharg. So bad was their reputation that, when they turned up in Ireland, they spelled their name backwards as a disguise. As if that was fooling anybody.

But long after the Border itself went off the boil, the old folk ways continued in the Anglo-Irish and Scots-Irish communities of Ulster, many of whom had come from the Borders. They reverberated in the rattling Orange Order marching bands and the salvoes of balaclavaed Republican honour guards. There was a memory of them in the back-street knee-cappings and the revenge killings in the Maze. Visit what the army called the badlands of Armagh or watch the demonstrations at Drumcree and you'll find the reivers.

At the end of the wood the Scots Dike disappears altogether at the top of a rise overlooking the River Esk. A place marked today for some unaccountable reason by what I assume is meant to be a sculpture. A couple of hundred yards further on the Border crosses the A7 at a charmless lay-by, the location for this year's England–Scotland litter international. The Scottish Borders Tourist Board has put up an interpretation sign advertising a tower in Hawick, Sir Walter Scott's courtroom in Selkirk and the Midlothian mining museum. The Border isn't mentioned.

Below us in the fields by the river you can find, appropriately enough, two faces of the Grahams. There's Kirkandrews Tower, one of their blunt fortified peles with its barrel-vaulted ground-floor chamber into which cattle could be driven in times of trouble. On the floors above was space for the extended family to take refuge if they found themselves under attack from the Bells or the Maxwells from Scotland or on the receiving end of a retributive raid by the English Lord Warden. If the Grahams had ever been tempted to advertise one of their pele towers for sale they'd have been able to claim with some justification that it was little used by the one careful owner because, mostly, they were away attacking somebody else. Kirkandrews Tower was gentrified a bit in Victorian times but still has an ominous scowl.

Then across the park there's Kirkandrews church – 'not at all a villagey job', as Pevsner rather snootily describes it in his *Buildings of Cumberland and Westmorland*. It was built in 1776 as the estate church for Netherby Hall, the family's stately pile across the river. Its columned rotunda and Italianate interior stand as testimony to the Grahams' capacity to survive and prosper. Demonized and deported in the early seventeenth century, within twenty-five years they'd crept back and were hiding out in the wastes of Bewcastle. You can't keep a bad man down. One Richard Graham, who'd harnessed his reiving skills as Master of the Horse to the Duke of Buckingham, bought the Netherby estate and the Barony of Liddel from the Duke of Cumberland and was created a baronet – Richard Graham of Esk – in 1629. His grandson was elevated to the peerage of Scotland as Viscount Preston and was Ambassador to the Court of France for many years. By the nineteenth century they were as establishment as you could get. Sir James Graham, Bart., of Netherby became Home Secretary. Kirkandrews church, where the later, grander Grahams are buried, is a symbol either of sinners coming to repentance or, more likely, of the Grahams flaunting the benefits of the peace dividend that eventually flowed from the Union of the Parliaments and which they'd carefully positioned themselves to get their hands on.

But inside the porch of their church at Kirkandrews there's a stone on which is carved a double-handed sword. It's tempting to suggest that even in their glory days the Grahams were hedging their bets.

At low water in the River Esk just across from Kirkandrews Tower it's still possible to find the remains of one of the most contentious bits of building anywhere on the Border. Nobody knows when the fish garth on the Esk was first built by the English, but we do know that by 1474 the Scots had demolished it. It was a sandstone dam and weir designed to hold migrating salmon south of the Border in English water. Commissions galore tried to arrive at a cross-Border compromise. In August 1494 one such met at the Lochmabonstone 'to put a final end to the controversy as to the fish garth'.

It didn't. The little weir on the Esk became a running sore in relations between the English and Scots Crowns, forever being pulled down and rebuilt. 'Aye, it was up and doon mair aften than a hoo-ers drawers,' as one helpful local told me.

It had become a point of principle. So much so that, shortly before the battle of Flodden, James IV of Scotland challenged the English commander Thomas Howard, Earl of Surrey, to single combat. The stakes? If the King won he expected, first of all, the removal of the fish garth on the Esk and then, apparently less important, the restoration of Berwick to Scotland. So far as we know that fight never took place. Unfortunately for King James and for Scotland, Flodden did. But on that occasion, at least, the fish garth wasn't what they were fighting about.

But the salmon continued to cause bother, according to a footnote in Sir Walter Scott's *Redgauntlet*. In the eighteenth century the Grahams of Netherby, by then having transformed themselves from criminals into the local gentry, again laid claim to the fishing rights on the Esk and again rebuilt the fish garth.

The Scots people assembled in numbers by signal of rocket-lights and rudely armed with fowling pieces, fish spears and such rustic weapons, marched to the banks of the river for the purpose of pulling down the dam-dike objected to. Sir James Graham armed many of his own people to protect his property and had some military from Carlisle for the same purpose. A renewal of the Border Wars had nearly taken place.

There was much rowdy posturing on both sides, but eventually Sir James backed off and agreed to put a breach in the dam to allow the passage of fish. Not that disputes over the salmon entirely ended there. As the Grahams of Netherby also tended to be chairmen of the local Bench, poaching was treated as the most serious of anti-social activities. Sadly, as is so often the case, the national law was out of touch with local sentiment and neither flogging nor transportation was permitted as punishment.

Occasionally, though, the Grahams would take a rather more benign view of poaching. That was when the big house was playing host to a particularly incompetent bunch of angling guests who'd paid several hundred pounds a week for the privilege of catching bugger all. They'd been promised a grand dinner of salmon to round off their stay and red stuff out of a tin just wouldn't pass muster. So a keeper from Netherby was despatched to the Globe Tavern in Longtown to collect Poody, who was, allegedly, the finest local practitioner of the poacher's art. Salmon were swiftly provided, the dinner was saved and Poody bought drinks all round for the rest of the night. Debateable Land pragmatism still alive and well in the 1970s. Among Poody's drinking companions was a man with one leg, whose name I've forgotten, who used to ride his one-pedal bicycle to the pub loo. But that's got nothing to do with this story at all.

Longtown has. Just three miles into England, it provides an insight into the business of the Border. The locals speak with one of the strongest of all Cumbrian accents. Visitors from Langholm, just ten miles to the north, speak in impenetrable

Scots. The accent changes at the Border line despite the fact that for centuries these people have lived in or robbed each other's pockets. Somebody once tried to explain the phenomenon by suggesting it was the school playground that perpetuated the accent but I prefer to think that it comes from the same sense of place and belonging that keeps Longtown wick with Grahams and Hetheringtons and Nixons while Langholm is foo of Maxwells and Irvines and Johnstones.

I was told in Langholm that nobody there would consider having their babies in the posh new hospital in Carlisle because that would taint them English. There was also a suggestion, vaguely supported by anecdotal evidence, that the people of Langholm tended to come home to die so that they could be buried on Scottish soil. The people of Longtown are more relaxed about these things. Like all the English they have less of a sense of belonging, but I still remember one night in the Bush pub in Longtown when somebody was refused a drink because he was an Armstrong.

The profound differences in language and habit on either side of an otherwise imperceptible Border reminded me for some unaccountable reason, as I stood in Longtown's main street, of something Graham Greene experienced when he did his *Journey Without Maps* through the forests of West Africa. In 1935 he set off to walk across Liberia on a meandering journey that, from time to time, shambled across the border into what was then called French Guinea. There wasn't a border, just more of the same. More trees and more impenetrable undergrowth. But the minute the non-border was crossed Greene noticed that the architecture changed and that the women were more beautiful, as you'd expect from women with French connections. 'They . . . lived up to the standard of a country which provides the handsomest whores and the most elegant brothels. The country was stamped as French from the first village we stayed in . . . You could not have mistaken this land for Liberia.'

So far as I'm aware both Longtown and Langholm are devoid of brothels, elegant or otherwise, but you still couldn't mistake Langholm for an English town.

When I used to go courting in Longtown the place was known as Dodge City. In those days, fights at Saturday night dances in Longtown Memorial Hall were the stuff of legend. The Western SMT bus company would ship in coachloads of Scottish reivers from Gretna and Eastriggs and then retire to a safe distance while the grudges of five hundred years were re-enacted.

But just along the road from the Memorial Hall, on a hill overlooking the River Esk, is the place that originally established Longtown's troublesome credentials long before the reivers were even a glint in the evil eye. Arthuret is the site of a battle in the sixth century where legend and history clashed. In the blood and mist of that battle were omens of the chaos that would lead to the overthrow of the British Celtic kingdoms. The resulting power vacuum was filled by advancing invaders and eventually, inexorably, the creation of a front line between two brand-new countries that became the Border itself.

At Arthuret in 573 the Christian king of York defeated the pagan ruler of Carlisle. So terrible was the bloodshed that a local bard called Myrddin (he probably wasn't a very good bard, given that his name translates as 'the little shitty one') was driven mad and ran for his life into the forest of Caledon, where poets eventually rescued his memory and recreated him as the wizard Merlin. But in the immediate aftermath of the battle of Arthuret another hero emerged from the bloody ruins. King Urien of Rheged, a kingdom that rose from that defeat to stretch from south-west Scotland to north Lancashire, was a Christian warrior and a consummate cavalry general. He probably led the last, desperate and eventually unsuccessful campaign against the advancing Anglo-Saxons in the north. An early history[6] suggests he almost won, but jealousy among the British leaders led to his assassination. Whoever he was, whatever happened to him, he's come down to us with another name. Urien of Rheged, so it's said, was the inspiration for King Arthur. Here at Arthuret (a place name which, just to make things really difficult, has nothing whatsoever to do with Arthur), the legendary circle closes. Merlin and Arthur are reunited in a patch of Cumbrian dairy pasture.

Having escaped from Longtown rather more easily than it can escape from its reputation as a battle zone and a Wild West frontier town, at Kirkandrews we bounce across the river on the slender and clanking Heath Robinson suspension bridge built by the Grahams to connect the family church with Netherby Hall. I wouldn't like to make the crossing in a high wind. The Border runs a few hundred yards north along the Esk from Kirkandrews churchyard to a place called the Willow Pool, where it takes to the Liddel Water. And the Liddel is a seriously pretty stream, meandering and chuckling under trees that dip to the water. But for many years it was the red river flowing out of what was the bloody cockpit of the Border troubles. Liddesdale was the territory of the Armstrongs and the Elliots, sometimes sturdy allies, sometimes pragmatic enemies of the Grahams.

The Armstrongs, who styled themselves a Scottish family, were probably from Cumberland. They were the worst of the worst when it came to theft and general mayhem. It's been claimed, I suspect fancifully, that they were capable of mustering upwards of 3,000 men. What is certain is that for four centuries they ran rings round the English and Scots

6 Nennius, *History of the Britons* (ed. J.A. Giles), Henry G. Bohn, 1848

authorities. The phrase 'a law unto themselves' could have been invented for the Armstrongs.

The Elliots were a smaller mafia but perfectly formed as a fighting force. They were definitely Scottish but still happy to accept English protection and English brass when it suited them. Which was usually when they'd fallen out big style with one of their Scottish neighbours. Which was most of the time. There are frequent references to Elliot raiding parties of more than a hundred riders.

As we've touched on the numbers game, it's worth making the point that quite a lot of the claims made about how many people the riding families could put in the saddle are probably overblown. Scraps of tavern embroidery. The same goes for the size of armies in the Middle Ages. Most medieval battles between the English and Scots were relatively small-scale affairs involving nowhere near the tens of thousands of troops that have sometimes been described by chroniclers who naturally wanted to embellish a good tale. To put the whole thing into some sort of perspective, the entire population of England was less than three million in the early 1500s and still under five million by 1600. Places like the Debateable Land were overcrowded because a lot of villains had huddled together for mutual protection, but the rest of the countryside was sparsely populated with perhaps only twenty or, at the very most, thirty people to the square mile and vast tracts of mountain and moorland with virtually no population at all. It's very hard to calculate what the total population of the Borders was in the mid-sixteenth century. Some people have tried. D.L.W. Tough[7] trawled the muster rolls of the English Marches for 1584 and came up with a figure of 120,000 people in the

7 D.L.W. Tough, *The Last Years of a Frontier*, Oxford University Press, 1928 (reprinted Sandhill Press 1987)

whole of the English Borders. The equivalent Scottish calculation is even harder to make, but he thought the figure might be somewhere about 45,000. Other methods of working out the sums give a population as low as 19,000. And that's the entire Scottish Borders, and it includes women, children and old people. For the Armstrongs, just one of almost thirty Scottish riding families, to assemble 3,000 fighting men at short notice just doesn't sound feasible.

Taking the opposite tack to the chroniclers who probably inflated the figures to emphasize the power of the reivers, I think the impact of families such as the Armstrongs of Liddesdale was even more impressive if you suggest they achieved their notoriety with 300 men rather than 3,000.

The front door of Liddesdale is guarded on the English side of the river by Liddel Strength, one of the finest motte-and-bailey fortifications in Britain. Because it's in Liddesdale it's scarcely visited. A keep, originally topped by a wooden palisade and defended by deep, sheer ditches and outer baileys, it was built by forgotten Normans as part of their conquistadorial campaign to subdue the north. By 1165 it was in the possession of the Scottish king, William the Lion, who granted it to Jedburgh Abbey, but by 1300 it was back in English hands, one of Longshanks' listening posts on the northern frontier and a jumping-off point in his campaigns to hobble Scotland.

In the middle of the fourteenth century it was controlled by Edward III's constable, Sir Walter Selby. With a garrison of just 200 men he held out for some days against the full force of David II's invading Scottish army. When it was eventually taken, Selby was made to watch while his two sons were strangled before he, too, was butchered and thrown from the battlements.

My arrival at the place which is also known as the Mote of Liddel coincided with a party of jolly hockey sticks hikers who seemed to have come armed with rather more reference books than was good for them. Their ever so knowledgeable leader was in full flow about the iniquities of industrial capitalism – an interesting line of argument in the context of a fortified Norman earthwork. Until I gathered he was complaining about the Victorian entrepreneurs who'd desecrated a great monument by building their railway line at the foot of it. We were standing on the abandoned track bed of the Waverley line. My little contribution to the debate – that to be able to build the railway they'd diverted the course of the Liddel which, until then, had been threatening to undermine the motte and bailey and wash it down the river – seemed not to make his day. Ho hum. But while I had the upper hand I told his fresh-faced, bright-eyed little party about the grisly murder of the Selbys in Technicolor detail before waving them a cheery goodbye.

As I headed off towards Penton it occurred to me I'd better include a word or two about rights of way. The Border line isn't a public footpath, which I suppose goes without saying, given that for quite a lot of the way it runs up the middle of rivers and streams. Bits of it are – those stretches that cut across open access moorland and through amenity forest. Further east there are some sections of the Border line running through territory that's debateable to this day, which would make the basis of an interesting trespass case (but only in England, there being no trespass law in Scotland). But there are some sections where the landowners are as territorial now as they were in 1552. The KEEP OUT signs should give you a clue. And whatever you do, don't say Eric Robson sent you. The Robsons (originally the wild men of Tynedale) still have a bit of a reputation in these parts.

CHAPTER FOUR

Viaduct on the Waverley Railway

iddesdale was where the skills of the Border reivers were honed to perfection. It was said of them that 'If Jesus Christ were emongest them, they would deceave him', these Borderers with no knowledge of the sixth and eighth commandments. Not that Christianity had passed them by. There's evidence it had taken root in Liddesdale a thousand years earlier. A squad of dry stane dykers, repairing a collapsed field wall in the valley, came across a stone inscribed in Latin to mark the final resting place of Carantus, son of Cupitanus. It was dated to the fifth or sixth centuries. As it was more than six feet long and weighed getting on for a quarter of a ton, it wasn't the sort of thing that you'd pop on your shoulder while trolling about the countryside. And Liddesdale certainly isn't short of walling stone. Who Carantus was and how he ended up by a roadside in Liddesdale we'll never know, but the Latin inscription on his headstone suggests he was Christian.

Nominally the reivers were God-fearing folk, too. They just had a different arrangement with him. And their rather mixed-up relationship with God's church on earth leaves us another, more robust inscription. This time the famous curse laid on the reivers by the Archbishop of Glasgow, Gavin Dunbar, in 1525.

I curse thair heid and all the haris of thair heid; I curse thair face, thair ene, thair mouth, thair neise, thair toung, thair teith, thair crag, thair schulderis, thair breast, thair hert, thair stomok, thair bak, thair wame, thair armes, thair legges, thair handis, thair feit, and everilk part of thair body, frae the top of thair heid to the soill of thair feit, befoir and behind, within and without . . .

And another couple of pages in similar vein. Gavin Dunbar was the Pope's representative in Scotland and his curse was the sixteenth-century equivalent of the UN slapping a resolution on Saddam Hussein ordering him to give up his weapons of mass destruction. The principal difference was that the reivers had some and could mobilize them in forty-five minutes.

But the really interesting thing about the curse on the reivers is the way it's retained its power down the centuries. As part of their millennium celebrations Carlisle commissioned an artist to inscribe part of the curse on a ten-ton boulder to be put on display in the city's Tullie House museum. The bit of installation art cum historical oddity attracted scarcely a mention until a local councillor blamed its malign influence for everything from an outbreak of foot-and-mouth disease to floods in the city and the burning down of a local bakery. According to him and a bunch of fundamentalist Christians who got in on the act, the reivers may have been gone for centuries but the evil they brought to the place lingers on.

The Armstrongs and the Robsons would have liked the thought of their curse making it on to CNN and Sky News. They always revelled in their bad reputation. But even though they were deeply superstitious, they'd still have thought the councillor and his Alleluia pals were crackers.

The reivers were practical men. They stole and they murdered, they kidnapped and they burned. They were operating sophisticated protection rackets five hundred years before Al Capone learned to take candy with menaces from the baby in the next pram. The traveller John Udall, who spent a couple of months on the Border in 1598, saw the Borderers as brutal savages whose ambition was limited to base subjects, just like carrion crows. But the people of the Borders considered themselves to be honourable – after a fashion. There are innumerable stories in the Border records of the very worst offenders sticking to their word. In 1596 one Widow Smyth of Lanercost paid protection money to the Grahams. When they next raided her village they 'inquired where the widow who paid blackmail dwelt and harried all the rest except her.' She escaped the raid, but hers being the only house left standing in the village can't have done much for relations with her neighbours. If the reivers had a colourful and much-trumpeted sense of honour, what they certainly didn't have were airs and graces. It wasn't their fault that Sir Walter Scott applied the spit-and-polish treatment and gave them a romantic bearing and heroic stature.

The derivation of the word reiver is ancient. A 'reef' in Old English meant a line. Later a 'Shire Reeve' was a man who protected an area's boundaries. We still call a person who travels across borders a rover. The reiver raided across the Border Line.

And the reivers left a number of words in the language, most of them sinister or sad. Their criminality led to the words bereaved and bereft. They gave us blackmail, and there are two suggested origins of that word. Apparently greenmail was a sort of agricultural rent and blackmail was the rent taken by night, in other words protection money. The other suggestion is that the word comes from the fact that decent men took pride in their gleaming armour. The reivers blacked theirs to ride as shadows in the moonlight. They practised 'boggling' or 'bauchling', the hurling of insults to encourage the duel or the feud and the derivation of our phrase 'mind-boggling'. The reiving families were known as 'graynes' and any member who offended against the family rules would be expelled for 'going against the grayne'.

Reiving behaviour has even had benefit of intense academic scrutiny. I recently stumbled across an American anthropological journal which claimed that at the heart of reiving was what it described as Stage 1 and Stage 2 warfare.

> Reiving, like all Stage 1 war, was for the purpose of getting loot, of obtaining goods 'by the shedding of a little blood', to paraphrase Tacitus.

Their feuds, though, were Stage 2 warfare.

> Stage 2, 'display warfare', as practised by many tribal peoples, has a sick sense of balance at its core; the desire to get even; the feeling that if your side falls behind in the murder derby, you are in 'spiritual decline'. In a land where resources are scarce, where violent attack might come at any time, to fall behind, to be seen as the weaker party, was to invite bullying from other parties – exactly as one might challenge a weakening big man, hoping to take his place. The best defence, for big man or Reiver grayne, was to seem fearsome, to be fearsome, so that only a fool would dare try to risk an attack. [8]

So, like the Maori when engaged in their warrior displays, the Zulu with their choreographed fear-making or the natives of Papua New Guinea in their cannibalistic excursions, the reivers were just demonstrating a tribal quirk. I wonder if they realized.

A short walk along a riverbank in Liddesdale doesn't give us sufficient time to do proper justice to the reivers. To get to know the men in leather jerkins riding into the night on their hardy pricker ponies – Nebless Clem Crosier and Banepryke, Buggerback and Archie Fire the Braes – you need to arm yourself with a copy of George MacDonald Fraser's majestic book *The Steel Bonnets*. He allows you to look into their bloodshot eyes. He lets you smell their breath and their

8 P.J. Nebergall, *Journal of World Anthropology*, University at Buffalo, 1996

presence. He makes them speak. Anyone who's daft enough to try to outdo George Fraser in reiver territory deserves a torch in the thatch.

But I'm still going to have my three pennyworth.

My view, for what it's worth, is that the reivers have been treated a bit unfairly by history; that they didn't deserve quite so bad a press. We certainly need to strip away Sir Walter Scott's romantic varnish, but I think that to write the reivers off as dim thugs and rustic psychopaths is a mistake. Reviled for their violence and criminality, they were also renowned for their music, much of it songs about the daring exploits of their forefathers. Music which could move judges and enemies alike 'if not to pity, at least to wonder vehemently'.[9]

For more than four centuries the Borderlands were seen as the scrag end of their respective countries, the frayed edges of monarchy. English borderers and Scottish borderers at least had that much in common. The Border was a remote battleground where national ambitions could be fought over. Northumberland, Durham, Cumberland and Westmorland were excluded from the Domesday Book. They were regarded as a military buffer zone. They became a bearpit.

It goes without saying that religion, too, played its part in destabilizing Border society. In the late fourteenth and early fifteenth centuries England supported the Pope in Rome, Urban VI, while Scotland, ally of the French, adhered to Clement VII, the anti-pope as he was known, enthroned in Avignon. In 1385 Richard II led a vast English army across the Border, burning the outposts of 'the enemies of Christ's cross' at the abbeys of Melrose and Dryburgh. In retaliation Franco-Scots forces raided as far south as Cramlington and Ovingham in the east and Cockermouth in the west, causing

9 J. Leslie, *History of Scotland*, Scots Text Society, Edinburgh, 1888–95

much damage. Quite what the good residents of Cumberland and Roxburghshire were asking for in their prayers and whom they were asking is anybody's guess, but you can bet your life that whoever was listening would be hard pressed to satisfy everybody.

Bottom line is that it was great men and grand schemes that got the Border into a mess long before the reivers took to the saddle. Any excuse would do. Armies came and went, practising their scorched-earth skills on the way. When the armies withdrew, cross-Border raids were encouraged to grind down the resolve of such defence forces as remained. Life for the people of the Border was hellish, and sensible men change their lifestyle if they find their backyard has turned into a war zone. The Borderers learned to get up and go, to have forms of wealth that were easily transportable – like sheep and cattle. They reckoned to be able to build themselves a house in a day. They knew the wild places where they could hide themselves and their black cattle until danger passed. They learned how to travel quietly at night across vast distances to keep out of the clutches of military scouting parties and government spies. But they still had to watch their children trampled, their wives abused and their old people left out to die in bitter Border winters. The law, such as it was, failed to protect them and they turned their backs on it.

The violence certainly wasn't a one-way traffic. A report gleaned by D.L.W. Tough[10] in his study of the later Elizabethan Border suggests that the Wardens, the law officers, could be every bit as brutal as the reivers when it came to the treatment of prisoners.

10 D.L.W. Tough, *The Last Years of a Frontier*, Oxford University Press, 1928 (reprinted Sandhill Press 1987)

Which prisoners hath been also extremely tortured and pinched, by thrusting hot irons into their legs and other parts of their body, and fettering them naked in the wilderness and deserts by chains of iron to trees, whereby they may be eaten up with midges and flies in summer and in winter perished with extreme cold . . . with sundry other unchristian devices to compel them to promise greater ransoms.

The experience of living in this dog-eat-dog Borderland bred valuable survival skills. The riding families learned how to play the system and turn brutality and international chaos to their own advantage. They offered their expertise to the highest bidder. And when the armies went home, they went back to their day job. A job as structured and bound by clearly defined rules of conduct as that of the bank manager, the accountant and every other professional engaged in the business of robbery. Every family on the Border knew the score and most gave as good as they got. It was a way of life, originally forced on them, which many got to enjoy. And because they found a way of beating the system they survived. The butcher in Newcastleton is still an Elliot, the Scotts of Buccleuch still own 227,000 acres of the Borders and the descendants of the feud-addicted Kerrs of Cessford are still living in Floors Castle at Kelso, the largest inhabited house in Scotland, as the Dukes of Roxburgh. The boys did good.

We've walked along the River Liddel past Riddings, where there used to be a junction on the Waverley railway. A branch line to Langholm was carried high across the river on a stately viaduct which still stands draped in weeds and saplings like some decrepit Borders equivalent of the hanging gardens of Babylon. The Langholm branch railway was still carrying homeward-bound reivers as late as the 1960s. On 'Simmer Fair Nicht' they'd catch the train from Riddings on their way to the

Common Riding, where they'd act out the rituals of five hundred years ago. Feats of horsemanship would be re-enacted as they rode the bounds of their territory. Family would be celebrated, old skirmishes remembered around tables awash with beer and whisky.

One morning after the celebrations the return train on the Langholm branch managed to set off on time but the engineman forgot to hook up the coaches. He got halfway to Riddings before he noticed and had to nurse his hangover back to Langholm to pick up the rest of the walking wounded. The old-time reivers held their drink better.

Across the River Liddel there's Rowanburn, one of three places on the Border where they mined for coal on an industrial scale – the original reason for the branch line. The rows of miners' cottages are still there. And the spoil heaps. I'm afraid they offended Logan Mack mightily. 'It is not generally known that within a short distance of this lovely stretch … coal-pits exist and miners' houses abound. Fortunately they are not in evidence, being situated in a hollow, and they do not therefore disturb the beauty of the surrounding country.' He would doubtless have been delighted to hear that industrial Rowanburn has now been reclassified as a brownfield site suitable for the erection of desirable country residences. The pit heaps are being levelled. But quite what the new, upwardly mobile residents of Rowanburn will make of the monstrous statue of a Border reiver gracing the main street I know not. It looks as if it was carved with a chainsaw by a blind man the worse for drink.

And then further along the river we get to Penton Linns, by contrast one of the most beautiful places on the Border line. The peat-brown water runs through deep pools and over shallow waterfalls in a geologists' paradise of deeply eroded rock strata. Late afternoon sunlight shimmers through the canopy of trees. My mum and dad used to bring me here for picnics on breathless summer Sunday afternoons, driving out from Carlisle in our Standard Flying Fourteen (which eventually I managed to send to the scrapyard by snapping off a plug in the block). I'd play in the pools on the river while Dad constantly warned me about the dangers of drowning and Mum made the sandwiches. I never did work out why she made the sandwiches on location, balancing slices of bread on her knee, rather than at home before we left. Even from this distance I remember afternoons at Penton as one of the most beautiful interludes of childhood. But don't be fooled by appearances. This is where the bloody suppression of the western Border began.

In 1552, just after the Debateable Land was carved up and when the officials were patting themselves on the back about how clever they'd been, there was an upsurge of violence here that rocked the Border. To try to contain it, more than sixty men with bloodhounds were formed into night watches to patrol this short stretch of the frontier along the Esk and the Liddel. By day they'd patrol the high places. At night, from 1 October to 16 March each year, they guarded river crossings. They were stood down through spring and summer when 'trade' was slack. I imagine the reiving families of the area treated the new system as a bit of a joke. But for all its blundering inadequacy it was another stone in the wall of international co-operation that would eventually hem the reivers in.

However, for the time being it was business as normal. After the battle of Langside in 1568, when the army of the abdicated Mary, Queen of Scots was routed in forty-five minutes and she made the fatal mistake of bolting for England, the reiving families celebrated by stepping up the mayhem. So the following year the Scottish Regent, the Earl of Moray, took the reivers on at their own game. Working in collaboration with the English Warden, Sir John Forster, he marched into Liddesdale and burned every house. Standing at Kershopefoot and looking along the valley across the centuries, you can still imagine the cheers of the Armstrongs and the Elliots when, two years later, news arrived of the Earl of Moray's murder, the first recorded assassination by a firearm. And when the cheering stopped they probably decided they'd better lay in supplies of this grand new technology.

But the pace was quickening. On 29 July 1567 a thirteen-month-old baby had been crowned King of Scotland in the sombre surroundings of the church of the Holy Rood in Stirling. And that baby's whimpers and cries were probably caused by the wind of change. Baby James was the son of Mary, Queen of Scots but, more important, after his mother's execution he would be the nearest living relative of the unmarried and childless Queen Elizabeth of England through his descent from Margaret Tudor, the sister of Henry VIII. We'll be back in her company at the far end of the Border.

James VI of Scotland was the front-runner for the English throne and English officials along the Border knew it. A new spirit of cross-border co-operation developed. After all, the last thing they wanted was to annoy the new boss. In his twenties James began to turn his attention to the raggedy seam between what would, one day, be his two kingdoms – the place he would eventually call his Middle Shires. He is often portrayed as effeminate and scholarly but that wasn't the side of him the Borderers saw. Time and again his forces harried Liddesdale and the old Debateable Land, and James was at their head. He was accused by families like the Grahams of robbery and slaughter on a grand scale. When he withdrew, the trees along the Liddel hung black with corpses.

In 1597 he came back and George Fraser reports a letter he wrote to Henry Leigh, the English Deputy Warden of the West

March, setting out his plans: 'We have resolved to passe forward in proper person uppon them with fyre and sword upon Tuesday next, to their extermination and wreike.' Such advance warning of a raid shows that the old fears of local connivance and betrayal had gone. James also wanted the English Warden's active assistance: 'and intreat yow that yow wilbe in a redynes with some sufficient force to remaine at the Mote of Lyddel . . . for hawlding them in at that syde.' In other words, while James crashed through the front door Leigh would have the back door locked to stop the men of Liddesdale escaping into England.

The only hanging corpses in Liddesdale today are of crows and magpies strung along a wire fence. But it's still a strangely silent valley, almost as if it's still not decent to be jolly in the company of so many ghostly reminders of its violent past. At Kershopefoot the border leaves the Liddel and takes to the Kershope Burn, which disappears into the forest. But that's tomorrow's challenge. This afternoon I'm going to walk further up into Liddesdale. And home to Newcastleton.

While I was reading Logan Mack's *The Border Line* I realized that he and I share a snapshot of Kershopefoot station. The locomotive of an Edinburgh freight is in Scotland, the brake van in England. And beside the train are the brightly coloured signs that the railway companies used to put up to mark the Border crossing.

Another snapshot. But one that Logan Mack never saw. A sad and shy man standing by the door of what looks like an army barracks. I've always thought of Kershopefoot as a rather sad place. Maybe it was the tales I was told as a little boy about the prisoner-of-war camp that used to be here by the river. And the unmarked graves of the German prisoners that never made it home and the forestry labour camp that took over from it and moved into its decrepit huts. Many of the timber

workers were refugees, like the man in the picture – Uncle
Ilko Stepan who escaped from the Ukraine at the start of the
Second World War and who bought me a wonderful model
aeroplane which I lost during a picnic at the Hermitage Burn.
Not that he was my uncle. Just that he married Aunt Agnes,
who wasn't my aunt. In fact she was the district nurse in
Newcastleton, and she managed my rather reluctant progress
into the world on New Year's Eve 1946.

For years after we changed countries and moved to
cosmopolitan Carlisle to live – that was when I was five – I
would spend every summer staying with Aunt Agnes at her
little cottage at the foot of the village. She was a kind and
powerful lady, marked down for spinsterdom in those days,
and her house smelled of blue and pink bath crystals. It was
on those visits that I got to know the other side of Liddesdale:
the tiny farms in the back of beyond, the shepherds' cottages
hidden in secret folds of the hills. I got to see the very
landscapes into which the reiver families would have retreated
when word came of an impending attack by King James or a
foray by the English Lord Warden Scrope from his castle in
Carlisle. Armstrong and Elliot women and children would
walk out to the Tarrass Moss, taking with them what few
possessions they could carry. Agnes and I and her border
terrier Roy went by Series E Morris and, when the road ran
out, tractor link box or pony. I'd sit wrapped in a blanket in a
low, pine-clad farm kitchen, hanging on to the dog and
listening to the hiss of the paraffin lamp while an anxious man
in tackety boots and trousers tied with baler string would rush
about boiling kettles on a peat-fired range. Just to keep him
out of the way.

And then the cry. Another generation of Borderer had made
it safely into the world. And then we'd be back in the link box
and on the way home through a grey dawn. Through the

wilder landscapes of Liddesdale that so entranced Sir Walter Scott. He came here every summer for seven years, exploring each ruined pele tower, tracing every stream to its source in the hills and gathering recollections of the songs and stories he would make famous. It was a primitive place even then. It looked as if it had scarcely recovered from its subjugation two hundred years earlier. Scott found no inn. He had to rely on the manse and local farmsteads for accommodation. He said that his horse-drawn gig was the first wheeled vehicle ever seen in the valley. But Scott was never one to let the facts get in the way of a good story.

The ballads he and others collected have thrown a velvet cloak of chivalry across the muddy puddle that was real Border history. Many of these stirring songs were first performed in the banqueting halls of the mighty Border families and so of course reflect their interests and etiquette. The gallant charge in the face of overwhelming odds, the fair lady in the castle tower awaiting the return of her valiant knight, the honours and dishonours of the medieval battlefield. The ballads promoted a cult of celebrity as irrelevant and superficial as the modern fascination with the excesses of third-rate singers and footballing personalities.

In Newcastleton they have a metropolitan chic bar in the Grapes now and the local builders have made a fortune doing up holiday homes – many of them for the English. Each July the village has one of the best traditional folk festivals in Scotland – liver damage set to music; and there's a golf course on the hill. And that's a real sign of progress. In 1457 James II of Scotland had 'gouf' banned because it was getting in the way of military training at a time when the country was under threat of English invasion.

The Newcastleton of my mind's eye hasn't changed at all. You look down on it from the Holm Hill and the smoke from its cottage chimneys still lies over it in layers of watercolour grey. A podgy little boy on a red and yellow tricycle is still taking Annie Jardine's three milk cows from their cobwebbed back-street byre out to the common grazings on the hill. And an older lad is still riding shotgun on Nuccan's horse-drawn cart (in those days I never thought to ask how you spelt Nuccan) that three days a week delivered coal and for two days collected the village rubbish to take to the old tip at the Pathhead. I can still remember being with my dad one New Year's Day, him singing and wearing a top hat decorated with tinsel and us both getting lost in the village where he'd spent most of his life.

I walked out to the Holm Hill past the station house where my mother had been born. Past the building that had been the isolation hospital where villagers had been sent to recover from TB and from where some didn't return. Past the deep, dark engine watering pond and the village bull pen which still had a bull in residence when I played out here, when I climbed up to peep fearfully over the wall and then run away when the creature put its great, sad head round the door of the old building.

I remember being told that the villagers used to hire a cowherd each year to look after their cattle at the common grazings on the hill. Village meetings would be held to decide who was the right man for the job. Everybody had a view, as they would in a community that had made its living out of liberating cattle for four hundred years. It was said that by comparison the election of the President of the United States of America was a simple matter.

On the seat at the top of the hill an old man, muffled against the chill, was taking the evening air. Purples and pinks flecked the sky away to the south. It was still and silent as Christmas Day.

'It's Eric, isn't it?'

'It is.'

'How's Nessie? Haven't seen her for years. Not since your dad died.'

'Oh, mother's cheery enough, but with Alzheimer's. Remembers every little detail about her life here as a girl but can't remember what happened ten minutes ago. She gets frustrated.'

'Maybe what happened ten minutes ago isn't as important. Least that's what I keep telling myself when I can't recollect what happened ten minutes ago. Anyway, before I forget, what brings you back to the Holm, Eric?'

I told him about the journey and the book I was writing and that I was trying to work out if the Border mattered these days. And he said the only border that he could see any sign of these days was between *Take the High Road* and *Coronation Street*.

'Television has rubbed us all flat,' was the way he put it.

Defensively I told him I'd given up defending the dumbing tendencies of television years back. 'But national pride, Scottish Parliament . . .'

A snort in the dusk. 'Scottish Parliament, English Parliament. All that's different is the architecture and I'm not sure which of that's better or worse, Victorian imperial or Costa del Holyrood. Not a one of them's got any real pride of place. They talk about Scottish independence, well, please God, no. Just imagine the meddling and tinkering they'd do if they got even a whiff of the airs and graces of being independent.'

Or words to that effect. So I asked him if he thought of himself as a Borderer first and foremost, and he said he supposed he did, but he was prepared to admit it's a bit of a cop-out. 'We've always called ourselves Borderers and said we were different somehow, but just as an easy excuse.' He said we used it as an excuse for the reiving long after the bad behaviour could be justified. And today it's an excuse for apathy. 'We say nobody understands us because we're remote and we're different. London doesn't understand us and the central belt of Scotland certainly doesn't understand us. But then when they ignore us, which is mainly what they do, we whinge about being the forgotten poor relations.'

'So that's the main similarity between English and Scottish Borderers, then. We're professional whingers. A bit harsh.'

'Aye, maybe. Put it down to the arthritis. But there's a grain of truth in it.'

As I set off back to the village he said, 'Tell Nessie that Geordie was asking after her.'

'That'll be Geordie the whinger?'

'Aye, that'll do.' But I didn't know which Geordie it really was and I didn't like to ask.

At the bottom of the hill Simmon's railway station has been bulldozed. There's a wire fence where the level-crossing gates used to be. It was here on a night in January 1969 that the Borderers of Liddesdale had their last hurrah. Led by their minister, the Reverend Brydon Mabon, playing his trombone, they blocked the level crossing in protest at the closure of their railway and stopped the midnight, the last scheduled train on the Waverley line. The minister was arrested. The young MP David Steel, who was travelling on the London-bound sleeper train, was got up in his pyjamas to negotiate the minister's release and persuade the crowd to let the train through. The next day British Rail staged a symbolic track-lifting ceremony at Riddings Junction to separate the London Midland Region from the Scottish Region. It was the end of what had been known as the Border Union Railway. Somebody said at the time that the British Railways Board had turned the clock back to 1602.

The closure of the Waverley killed one of the most isolated communities in Britain. Riccarton Junction was two stations up the line from Newcastleton and where the Border Counties Railway branched off the main line and headed for Hexham. The *Scotsman* newspaper described it as 'The Scottish equivalent of a wild west frontier town, a community created in the middle of nowhere to accommodate the arrival of the iron horse.' There were no roads to Riccarton. Access was entirely by railway for the 150 people who lived there. Grandfather Simon would send the doctor from Newcastleton by pilot engine if there was an emergency and if his treatment didn't work the coffin would come down to the village in the guard's van.

For all its isolation it was a lively place with its own pub – the Refresh, as it was known – and a grocer's shop and a school. And there were great dances. My mother and father did their courting on nights out by train to Riccarton. In its early days it was even livelier. The community was terrorized by four fearsome women. I bet they were Elliots. Peace was restored only when the railway company transferred their husbands to four different stations.

And old habits die hard. On the day the line closed in 1969 the Riccarton reivers had their own final fling. The last northbound train almost didn't make it to the top of the long haul from Riccarton to Whitrope Summit because the locals had greased the tracks.

Newcastleton is an example of the Borderers sticking together across generations and pecking orders. It dates from 1793 when the 3rd Duke of Buccleuch – only six or eight twigs down the family tree from the Bold Buccleuch immortalized in Border Ballad – gave land at the Copshaw Holm for the people of Liddesdale to build themselves a new, properly planned, village. But this wasn't Buccleuch emulating the brutal clearances of Strathnaver by the Sutherlands. This wasn't Bettyhill in the Borders. It was an attempt to lift people out of the poverty that had stalked the dale since the suppression of the Debateable Land. The Duke suggested they should supplement subsistence farming with handloom weaving. There was already a community of weavers north of the new village at Blackburnfoot who would walk the ten miles through the Tarras Moss to the Langholm mills with their warps and wefts slung across their shoulders. The houses lining Newcastleton's mile-long main street and its three squares were designed with extra-large front windows to let in the weavers' light. The model village was built but the plan failed. Liddesdale was just too far off the beaten track, as it always had been. But while it lasted the little isolated weaving community at Newcastleton apparently had quite a social conscience. Reiving families, social conscience – surely not? Well, apparently so. They organized regular concerts to raise money for cotton workers in the English mill towns and for north of England seamstresses whom they obviously thought were even worse off than them.[11] I'm sure the Buccleuch estates factor reported back to the big house about these revolutionary goings-on.

The intangible bond between the Border families still exists in many little ways. The Buccleuchs have a reputation for being good landlords; for knowing their tenants, many of whose families have been on that patch of land as long as the Buccleuchs themselves. When I first started making programmes for Border Television, I proposed a programme about the Buccleuchs and was invited to the big house at Bowhill to meet the 9th Duke. The programme went through on the nod. What the Duke really wanted to talk about was my grandfather, Mr Bell the stationmaster, and how kind he'd been to his father

11 Ann Charters and Betty Anderson, *Through the Eye of a Needle*, Liddesdale Heritage Association, 1993

one wet shooting day in the 1930s, and Mr Robson, who turned out to be Uncle Alexander (we knew him as Sned but the Duke couldn't be that familiar), who'd been a fencing ganger on the Buccleuchs' Langholm estate and had recently died.

And Sned was a true borderer. He drank in Scotland and he drank in England. His social life took him along the reivers' trails. When I first learned to drive and had a bone-shaking, clattering Land-Rover I'd pick him up from his bungalow in Newcastleton on Saturday mornings and go raiding with him. His legs had given up the ghost after years of standing knee deep in the Duke of Buccleuch's peat. But even on a Zimmer frame he'd make it to the pub. We'd start in the Grapes. It was neither metropolitan nor chic in those days. Then to the Commercial. It had been re-named the Liddesdale Hotel some decades earlier, but new names on old friends take a bit of getting used to. Next would be the High Corner in the hills beyond Kershopefoot. Its married name was the Dog and Gun and it was memorable for its less-than-fragrant soakaway outside toilet and the bottles of preserved snakes that adorned its bar. Sned would sometimes founder here and stretch out to sleep on the settle by the roaring fire to wait for a passing drinker who was heading in the general direction of Newcastleton. On wilder days the raid would go as far as Bellingham and Fourstones down the Tyne Valley. On the way Sned did a bit of cattle-dealing rather than rustling, but in most other respects he was merely updating the customs of the sixteenth century.

I walked on through the village, past the little corrugated-iron auction mart where, in my grandfather's day, the suckler sales gave a noisy reminder of the skills needed by the reivers to get their stolen cattle home. Suckled calves from the hill that had scarcely seen a human and that had been taken from their mothers that morning would be herded through the village to livestock pens at the station to be loaded into wagons for their onward journeys. They ran wild. The village school was shut for the day and the kids were kept indoors. But the Elliots and the Armstrongs of Newcastleton were a match for wild cattle.

And then on to Redheugh, the Liddesdale seat of the Elliots. Old Lady Elliot, who used to grace television coverage of the House of Lords by either sleeping on the red benches or waving her ear trumpet, is dead and the new head of the clan is the startlingly attractive Margaret Elliot, who would still be a match for wild cattle. We talked about reiving days rather in the way that you'd talk about Uncle Bill who you haven't seen for some years but wasn't he a card when he was a lad. We laughed about a hen that was trying to get in through the drawing-room window and compared notes about how badly roses do in cold, wet places. Reivers weren't always in the saddle. They had normal, mundane things to do too. But, on reflection, they probably didn't grow roses round the pele tower door.

When we were shooting the *Walking the Line* television series, Alistair Moffat and I went to see Margaret at Redheugh. Alistair was determined to cast reivers like the Elliots as hooray hooligans who deserved everything that was coming to them, and some. Margaret fixed him with a look that would have made Good Queen Bess blanch and explained in forensic detail the tribulations endured by her family during the black times. She talked of them as if they were cousins recently passed away. Margaret and Alistair agreed to differ, an option that wouldn't have been available in the 1570s. We'll have to wait and see how the Moffat/Elliot feud develops but if I was Alistair I'd keep well away from dark alleys for a bit.

Just beyond Redheugh is the junction with Hermitage Water. Turn left and you come to Hermitage Castle, to my mind the bluntest fortress in Britain. Standing 'roofless like a hollow tree that will not fall', as George Fraser describes it, it's a fist of masonry, a sod off in stone. Since the thirteenth century it's been putting the frighteners on the locals. It was widely believed that Hermitage was cursed and that the crimes of its owners were so great that the castle had sunk several feet into the ground under the weight of them. Maybe because of its unsavoury reputation, in 1960 the director George Schaefer picked Hermitage as a location for his movie version of *Macbeth*, which is credited with being the first ever made for TV. I remember my dad driving us up to the castle one bitterly cold night so that a starstruck teenage Robson could gawp at the arc lamps and the camera dollies and hope to catch a glimpse of Michael Hordern as Banquo and Ian Bannen as Macduff. The only person I recognized was a security guard from Carlisle who told us in best Hermitage tradition to sod off.

Turn right at Redheugh and in a mile or so you arrive at the earthworks of Liddel Castle plunging into the river. Another Norman stronghold in the badlands, it was built somewhere towards the end of the eleventh century by the Northamptonshire Baron Ranulph de Soulis.

By all accounts they were a bad lot, the de Soulis family. One of them even fired up the normally imperturbable James Logan Mack in *The Border Line*: 'If a tithe of the tales about his repute and actions are true he was indeed a fiend in human form.' He was talking about William, Lord Soulis, Keeper of Hermitage Castle and Sheriff of Roxburgh, who was taken out by his grateful people, wrapped in lead and boiled to death in a pot on the Nine Stane Rig. After which he apparently caused them no further trouble. It's a much-told tale but, sadly, like so many Border yarns, that's all it is. In 1320 Lord Soulis was convicted of conspiring against Robert the Bruce and banged up in the unsalubrious end of Dumbarton Castle where he died without need for boiling.

In the fields by Liddel Castle are the turf-covered humps and hollows which are all that remain of the original village of Castleton. It was always a poor place, made the poorer by the conflicts that raged around and through it. Its residents can't have shed many tears the day they abandoned it for good and moved two and a half miles down the valley to the new village. And I wonder what Edward I made of the place the night he stayed here in 1296 on his way from Roxburgh Castle to Carlisle. I assume he didn't join the locals in a bowl of gruel by the fire while they debated the parlous state of Anglo-Scottish relations. But maybe he did. He may have been the Hammer of the Scots but he was also a very modern monarch in lots of ways. He believed in a bond between a king and his people. And the fifty-seven-year-old Longshanks was probably in a jolly mood, having just thrashed the forces of John Balliol, the puppet king he'd set on the Scottish throne, who'd made the mistake of having delusions of independence. In fact Edward had goaded Balliol into rebellion to give him an excuse to confiscate Scotland. The plan worked but only in the short term. What Edward had created was Scotland, the implacable enemy, which, in alliance with France, would eventually cause England all manner of trouble.

But that evening as he sat at Castleton looking out over Liddesdale, Edward had Scotland as a vassal state at his back and a victorious England in front of him. William Wallace was still a year away from his revolt and the defeat of the English army at Stirling. The only flies were on the dinner, not yet in the ointment. Edward could look forward to another eleven years of hammering the Scots before the ague would get him at Burgh Marsh by the Solway Firth, where he died in 1307 just a cough and a spit away from the Border that defined his memory.

On his death bed Longshanks ordered that the flesh should be boiled from his bones, which were to be wrapped in a bull's hide and carried at the head of the English army every time the Scots tried to recapture their freedom. That was a bit agricultural for his son, the petulant, homosexual Edward II, and he had Longshanks' remains buried in Westminster Abbey instead. Very uninspired by comparison.

As I left Castleton there was a sunset from J.M.W. Turner. It dropped through a swirling abstraction of cloud and behind the elaborate memorials of Castleton cemetery. Orange to gold with a distant black fringe of thunder. I was tempted to stay until the light had completely gone; to imagine smoke drifting through the heather thatch of the black houses in the old village and the torches of riders on the hills across the valley. But there are ghosts at Castleton and you don't want to mess with them.

As I walked back to Newcastleton I passed the old, now abandoned, church where my parents were married one Valentine's day. From where they'd been driven back to the village in the wedding car past a rope barricade put up by the local kids and which they refused to take down until pennies were thrown. I was born the following December. Had I been born here in a different age, at my baptism one of my hands would have been wrapped in a strip of cloth to exclude it from the rite. At a time of blood feud that would have left me free in the eyes of God to strike unhallowed blows against my enemies. Quite what God thought of the arrangement isn't recorded. But recently I discovered that exactly the same ritual was practised by another border people, the Maniots from the Mani peninsula in southern Greece. They lived on the edge too. Constantly feuding, constantly at war with their own governments, they built their Greek equivalent of pele towers by the sea frontier that divided Turkish, Greek and Venetian spheres of influence in the Mediterranean. They were called Mavromichalis rather than Armstrong, but in most other respects they would have understood the ways of the Debateable Land very well.

CHAPTER FIVE

Kershope valley

Y ou find me trudging back to Kershopefoot after a jolly night of family reminiscences which involved much hammering of the Scotch. I've just set my body down to rest for a moment by the Millholm Cross on the road south from Newcastleton. The first body to be laid here, so it's said, was that of one of the leading Armstrongs of Liddesdale and he was in a worse state than me. His sons and brothers were carrying his corpse home following his murder by Lord Soulis in Hermitage Castle. They were heading for Mangerton Tower, just across the fields, which was the principal Armstrong residence in the valley. It's a heap of stones cut through by the track bed of the Waverley railway. But it was once one of the most feared places on the Border. Within its thick walls the Liddesdale reiving perfected their tactics. Hostages were held for ransom. From it raiding parties harried as far as Redesdale and Tynedale. Troublemakers swarmed to it, some for the protection of the Godfather, others to try their hand at knocking the great Armstrong from his perch. But for all its power and reputation, Mangerton sometimes fell to superior forces. Occasionally even the Armstrongs were outguiled.

When Logan Mack visited the ruins of the tower in the 1920s, he discovered an inscribed stone which was then just readable.

In the centre of this stone is a crest with an elbow inverted, the sign of the strong arm, otherwise Armstrong, having on one side of it the letter 'S' and on the other the letter 'A', doubtless indicating 'Sim Armstrong'. Those at the foot are clearly 'ER'. Now in 1363 the King of England was Edward III and at that time he had taken possession of Liddesdale. It may therefore be assumed that one of the Armstrongs, voluntarily or by compulsion, recognised Edward of England as his sovereign, instead of David II who was then on the throne of Scotland.

But if chipping the odd 'ER' above a door was all it took to hang on to their power base in Liddesdale, that wasn't going to exercise the Armstrongs greatly.

The 'Sim Armstrong' of Mangerton mentioned by Logan Mack was a family leader with Don Corleone tendencies. The tentacles of his control were far-reaching. He bought and sold lesser hoodlums. He knew what Lord Warden Scrope was having for breakfast in Carlisle Castle before the dish arrived in his apartments. But he met his match in Humphrey Musgrave, English Deputy Warden of the West March.

One of the jobs of the Deputy Warden was to 'follow the trod': to pursue reivers within six days of any offence being committed and to attempt to catch the perpetrators in possession of the stolen goods, 'red hand' – another Border phrase that passed into the language. Border law laid down strict rules about how the trod should be conducted. It should be no cloak-and-dagger affair. It had to be noisy with horns and hounds, led by a man with a flaming turf on his lance. They had to announce their intentions to the first person they met over the Border.

In 1584 the Armstrongs had been pillaging in Bewcastle. Deputy Warden Musgrave set off on their trail which, unsurprisingly, led to Mangerton. The details of the trod don't survive, but at the end of it Sim Armstrong was taken prisoner in Mangerton Tower and hauled off to Carlisle Castle, much to the amazement of the English authorities.

But it's what happened after Sim Armstrong's arrest that allows us to peep into the strange ways of Border administration. Old Sim was acknowledged to be one of the worst offenders in the area but within months he was back home at Mangerton. Presumably money changed hands. And in *The Steel Bonnets*, George Fraser turned up one of those historical asides that makes his understanding of the medieval

Border so vibrant. Apparently, a year after Armstrong's arrest, his captor, Humphrey Musgrave, entered a horse called Bay Sandforth in a race in Liddesdale because Sim of Mangerton wanted to see it perform. It won all three races and Armstrong bought it. Border law was important, but business was business. Sadly, no record exists of a later hot trod during which Sim of Mangerton outran Deputy Warden Musgrave on a fine horse called Bay Sandforth.

Within living memory the traditions of sporting Mangerton were still to be found. Liddesdale held Border games here in a meadow by the tower. Contestants would throw the 14lb hammer and put the 23lb ball. Great reiver training. And the gathering of Armstrongs and Elliots, Robsons and Grahams on the Mangerton meadow is as close as we'd get in modern times to one of the great days of truce held at nearby Kershopefoot and a handful of other acknowledged meeting places along the frontier during the centuries of Border aggravation.

The day of truce was a play within a play, a pantomime within a tragedy. And, like pantomime, it was performed to arcane and detailed rules. When the Lord Wardens representing the two countries arrived with their armed supporters – sometimes as many as three hundred on either side – it was a stand-off every bit as ritualistic as the close-up, narrowed eyes of Clint Eastwood or the adjusted stetson of Gary Cooper. The Lord Warden of the English March would send out an envoy: 'Either his deputy or some other special gentleman of good worth whom it pleaseth him to make choice of, with a convenient number of the best horsed and most sufficient gentlemen of his company.'[12] He would ask assurance from the Scottish Warden that they would all have

12 From a manuscript by Richard Bell, Warden Clerk of the Western March during much of Elizabeth's reign – in effect a Warden's handbook

safe passage. The Scottish Warden would raise his hand in assent and the envoy would ride back. A Scottish envoy and armed supporters would then ride across to the English side and repeat the process. When the Scots contingent had returned, the English Warden would announce the truce: 'Causeth proclamation to be made for observation of the peace . . . until the next day at the sun rising, upon pain of death.'

Once the Scottish Warden had responded with the same words, the English party would ride across into Scotland. And it was always done that way – perhaps a formalized nod in the direction of England's unsettled claims over Scotland. Perhaps, as Sir Robert Bowes suggests,[13] the Scots always sent their ambassadors into England first after a war to ask for peace, so it was only fair that at other times the English should return the compliment.

The English Warden would dismount and wait for his Scots counterpart to come to him. They'd then embrace and get down to business:'Draw themselves remote to some quiet place, interchangeably calling the rolls and bills of both sides in the presence of the gentlemen of the best sorts of both the countries.'

It was a stately gavotte in the wilderness, in which every detail of the proceedings was prescribed. Even the oaths were provided in an officially agreed form. A defendant would be required to 'Swear by heaven above you, hell beneath you, by your part of Paradise, by all that God made in six days and seven nights, and by God himself, you are whart out sackless of art, part, way, witting, ridd, kenning, having or resetting of any of the goods and cattels named in this bill: So help you God.'

And all this overlaid by an even more complex manual of Border laws – the Leges Marchiarum – which in turn were

13 Sir Robert Bowes, 'Account of the State of the Frontiers and Marches 1551', written at the request of the Marquis of Dorset, Warden General, British Library

amended by almost every treaty between the two countries. The Warden Clerk, the equivalent of the Clerk to the Court, must have had to travel to Kershopefoot with a full legal library to be able to rule on the complexities and legal niceties that could arise in even the simplest of cases. And given that both sides would have had a clerk, their inevitably conflicting interpretations of the law must have made the process of justice as cumbersome then as it is now. The Armstrongs and Grahams may have been known villains but they would often get away with it, and I bet there were people in Liddesdale or Tynedale who had cause to complain that the victims of crime were being ignored.

The problems were exacerbated by the power of the Warden himself – particularly the English Warden, of whom it was said that within his own March he was 'like a King of Israel during the absence of Elijah'.[14] He called the shots and if there were too many complaints lodged against his side he could put off holding days of truce for months, if not years. The complaints festered and the families with grievances took their own revenge.

But even during the worst of the bloodletting there was a rather touching naivety that ran through the reiving and feuding business. After one raid, in which a flock of sheep had been lifted, the thieves sent a note to their owners saying that the next time gentlemen came to take their sheep 'they were no to be scabbed'. How dare they leave a flock with sheep scab in a place where they could be nicked? Reivers, it seems, were easily offended.

They also had an odd sense of morality. Rather like the girl in the Tom Lehrer song who merrily carved up her family one after another but when the police came round immediately owned

14 Howard Pease, *The Lord Wardens of the Marches of England and Scotland*, Constable, 1913, limited edition

up because 'lying she knew was a sin', the reivers set great store by keeping their word and even telling the truth. A very large number of cases heard on days of truce were 'fouled by confession'. In other words, the offender came clean and paid his fine, which was probably something called 'double and sawfie', by which he had to pay twice the value of the stuff he'd pinched and a bit on top for court costs. Which, like as not, went straight into the Warden's back pocket. There was also an accepted scale under which the proceeds of ransom and blackmail were divvyed up. The leader of the raid got one-eighth and the other riders shared the rest. It was as well ordered a black economy as any you'll find being paid up in used notes in the back bar of a pub in Moss Side or Toxteth. The difference is that in the sixteenth-century Borderlands the policeman was often in on it. At least I hope that's the difference.

Before braving the Kershope forest, I needed to clear the hangover, and Windy Edge was just the place to do it. I climbed out to the 300-metre contour to the west of Kershopefoot to look for three monuments – two ancient and one relatively modern. When Logan Mack came out here he warned his readers to watch out for marauding wild bulls that wandered these hills. This morning they're bellowing inside my head.

The first memorial we come to is another cautionary tale. Here on the dividing line between Roxburghshire to the east and Dumfriesshire to the west, on 29 July 1805, one Michael Dixon of Castleton was struck by lightning. Quick check of sky. Mercifully cloud-free.

But trudge another five hundred yards across the moor through ankle-straining tussocks and you come to the house of the dead, the highest chambered cairn in Scotland built by Neolithic herdsmen around 3000 BC. Such cairns were places where the spirits of their ancestors were worshipped. Nobody knows what rituals were used as bodies were laid into the stone vaults, but the fact that so much effort went into the construction of these cairns shows how important the spirit world was to these early people.

Near by is the Bounder Stone, stripped by wind and weather, slumped at an angle in the peat but once probably part of a circle of great stones. It was a place where mystery and magic could be conjured, a place to which nomadic families would return at certain seasons of the year and near which they would eventually start to practise the revolutionary new techniques of agriculture. It's a reminder, if one were needed, that Liddesdale had a long and settled history of well-ordered tribal occupation and pastoral existence before progress in the form of brooding nationalism blew it apart.

Four and a half thousand years after it was first set up on Windy Edge, the Bounder Stone was pressed into service again. This monument to the spirit world was chosen to mark the northernmost tip of the Debateable Land; it was one of the specks in the landscape that the delineators of boundaries looked for as their compass points.

Looking out across the hills from the Bounder Stone you can see that these western Border landscapes are not spectacular. They don't have the sheared edges of Lakeland. The ice flattened them. At the end of the last Ice Age the melt waters broadened their river valleys. This is not a place to discover 'the picturesque'. Rather it's a blunt landscape that speaks its mind and tells of hard times rather than the good old days. As Camden reported in his *Britannia*, 'The country itself is mostly rough and barren and seems to have hardened the very carcases of the inhabitants.'

The English have a very strange view of landscape – a cross between a John Constable painting and a chocolate-box lid, as Howard Newby put it in his book *Green and Pleasant Land*.

They constantly hark back to a perceived golden age of thatched cottages and a happy peasantry on swaying haywains, ignoring the rats in the roof and the tuberculosis in the children. The northern Scots have an equally suspect attitude to their countryside. To them it's a Celtic netherworld, the land of the gods. Their bond with the landscape is almost aboriginal. The dreamtime. But in my experience the Borderer puts landscape in its place. It's merely a backdrop to more important things: something to do battle with rather than revere. That is not to say they won't defend it to the hilt if any incomer slights it. Just that among themselves it's unremarkable.

Like Kershopefoot. We're walking into the poor lands of Robert the Bruce. Well, they were his in 1304 and on a brooding wet morning, which is what it's become, it's tempting to say that the intervening centuries have not improved them. The river valley is a tree-lined meander of mature trees but beyond it is some of the hardest, wildest ground in Britain. Standing here in the rain, you have to wonder why they bothered fighting over the place for so many years. Particularly when you realize that for generations this ground had been considered worthless.

Until the early years of the thirteenth century the kings of England had regarded the northern extremities of their territory as expendable. Henry I, King Stephen, Henry of Anjou and Richard I had all happily given away bits of their northern territories to Scotland as a convenient way of dealing with political bother. Spending on royal castles was concentrated in Yorkshire – the 'inner core' of the north – rather than the front-line fortresses at places like Norham and Newcastle and Wark. But in 1204 something happened which suddenly made the ragged borderlands of northern England seem more important. England lost Normandy. The era of the absentee English monarch came to an end. English kings began to see the lands in the north as an alternative source of revenue and that's why, in the earliest-known document referring to this stretch of the Border, dated 9 November 1304, it was necessary to be specific about its boundaries.

An inspectimus by Robert the Bruce earl of Carrick and lord of Annandale, confirming the charter of his ancestor William de Rossedale who granted his land of Cresope by these bounds – The fosse of the Galwegians and the rivulus running from thence into Lydel, and on the other side of the fosse straight to the high moor, and so by the watershed of the moor as far as the old way of Roxburgh, and as said way falls into Cresope.

You had to set the boundaries before you could extract the rent.

Logan Mack reckoned that the tantalizing reference to the 'fosse of the Galwegians' probably referred to a mysterious trench which, in the 1920s, could still be found on Christianbury Crag four miles to the south and which could indicate an earlier Border line. We're going to make a detour to try to find it. And he thought 'the old way of Roxburgh' was most likely a reference to the Maiden Way (originally Maden or Madien, meaning simply a raised road) which long pre-dated the Roman occupation but beside which they built their fort at Bewcastle. If he was right, we should find evidence of it at a place called the Lamisik Ford, where the three old counties of Roxburghshire, Northumberland and Cumberland meet and where the ancient trackway supposedly crosses the Kershope Burn.

But before we drag ourselves away from the delights of rainy Kershope and tackle the next, considerably tougher bit of the walk, there's one other place to visit. Just a couple of hundred yards north of the village there's a little field trapped between the abandoned line of the Waverley railway and the River Liddel by the farm of Flatt. This was the Tourney Holme, known throughout the western Borders as the appointed place to stage single combat. If matters of honour were at stake, this strip of grass was the spot to have them satisfied. To the death. At a time when the courtly law of the Leges Marchiarum, as practised at days of truce in places like Kershopefoot, was seen to make it altogether too easy for criminals to walk free (a fundamental flaw of the system was that no Englishman was allowed to testify against a Scot and vice versa), a quick settlement of disputes by strength of arms was seen to be every bit as just. And if the concept of trial by combat sits unhappily with modern notions of justice handed down at arm's length, we should remember that trial by combat wasn't abolished in England until 1819, following the case of one Abraham Thornton. He was accused of manslaughter and elected to defend his cause 'by his body'. In the event the case was withdrawn, Thornton was set free and the ancient law which most people had forgotten was still on the statute book was abolished.[15]

The Tourney Holme at Kershopefoot was the setting for an episode in one of the great romantic yarns of Border history. In 1566 the Earl of Bothwell was Keeper of Liddesdale and Captain of the fortress of Hermitage. But above and beyond the call of duty he'd been putting in considerable overtime consoling Mary, Queen of Scots, who was becoming increasingly estranged from her reptilian husband, Lord Darnley. In the autumn of that year the Queen was in Jedburgh overseeing a dose of 'Jeddart Justice' in which offenders were hanged first and the finer points of their defence debated later.

15 Howard Pease, *The Lord Wardens of the Marches of England and Scotland*, Constable, 1913, limited edition

Bothwell decided to impress by supplying her with an assortment of Liddesdale hanging fodder. He rounded up a few troublesome Elliots and imprisoned them in Hermitage. But on his second sweep through the valley he came across Little Jock Elliot of the Park and challenged him to single combat on the Tourney Holme. Bothwell was brave and dashing and Jock Elliot was soon out of his saddle and on the ground. Bothwell strolled up to arrest the bold Captain. Now Jock Elliot may have been little and he may have been dying from his wounds, but he was a proper Border fighter. He waited until Bothwell was close enough and stabbed him three times – no doubt singing all the while a final rousing chorus of

My name is Little Jock Elliot,
And wha daur meddle wi' me?

The Keeper of Liddesdale had to be hauled back to Hermitage on a farm cart. To make matters worse, he then had the embarrassment of bleeding quietly outside the castle door because the Elliots had overpowered their guards and taken control. Presumably money changed hands and Bothwell got his castle back. And during his convalescence at Hermitage, Mary, Queen of Scots made what's sold in Border folklore as one of the most romantic royal journeys in history. On 16 October, in bad weather, she set out from Jedburgh with a group of courtiers and rode the twenty miles to Hermitage to bring comfort to her beloved Bothwell. Propriety meant she couldn't stay in the castle overnight, so after two hours of peeling grapes, rearranging the flowers and fluffing up the pillows she rode back, stumbling into a bog on the way and almost catching her death of cold. Romance in Border ballads should be taken with at least a pinch of salt and probably a hot toddy.

But the story gives me some justification for calling my soggy tramp up the Kershope Burn romantic. (Romantic – adj. Of, relating to, something stupid done in cold, wet weather.) Except it's a surprisingly pleasant walk if you half close your eyes and forget the driving rain. I'd been expecting an obstacle course of boulders and impenetrable thickets, which was what Logan Mack found in the 1920s. But this landscape has had two lives since then. Four years after *The Border Line* was published they started to plant one of the biggest man-made forests in Europe – 200 square miles containing 150 million trees – stretching from Kershope to the far reaches of Kielder. It would be a home-grown timber factory that would make sure we'd never again suffer the shortages of the First World War. But by the 1980s Sitka spruce had become environmental public enemy number two, after nuclear power stations. Chancellor Nigel Lawson scuppered the home-grown timber industry one afternoon when, in his budget, he got rid of the tax breaks that had encouraged well-known countrymen like Terry Wogan to plant trees on vast tracts of otherwise useless land such as the Flow Country.

There was a postscript to the Nigel Lawson story which shows that the old reivers' belief in standing up to overweening authority still survives and prospers. The present Duke of Buccleuch, passionate supporter of increased afforestation, was incensed by Lawson's change of policy. So he wrote to him and asked him to return, forthwith, the paintings – Canalettos or some such – which adorned his office walls in No. 11 Downing Street, loaned by the Duke's father to an earlier Chancellor, Sir Stafford Cripps. When the Duke told me the story the image that sprang to mind was of Mr Lawson trying to maintain his customary air of sullen pomposity while sitting at his desk in front of two less faded squares of wallpaper.

Anyhow, the Forestry Commission responded to these changed economic circumstances and to public pressure by starting to convert their forests into amenity woodlands. Now tourists are as important as timber production, which struggles to compete with world market prices anyway. The upshot is that the Kershope Valley, like the rest of the forest, is criss-crossed with waymarked Border trails for walkers and mountain bikers. Sitka has been cleared back from streams like the Kershope Burn to allow regeneration of native birch and rowan. Drifts of wild flowers, orchids and foxgloves, shine against a tumbling backdrop of dark peat water.

But they don't shine anywhere near as bright as the cyclists. A pack of them caught up with me by the Kershope Burn, all shimmering Lycra and heads that seem to point backwards. I can understand that in serious competition in the velodrome the slick of sheer fabric might give a racing advantage, but on the mud-ripping pedal to Larriston the only possible explanation is that it's a mating ritual. The bigger the bulges the better the mate you get. Unfortunately on this occasion there was a serious lack of females.

The bulk of the forest is in England. As far as the quarry at Kershope Bridge there's open land to the north, rising out to Caerby Hill. On some maps it's Carby Hill, but the local pronunciation is more accurate – Caerba, meaning the fortress of the ford. The top of the hill is defended by a great wall of stones more than a hundred feet in diameter which, in the second century AD, the Greek geographer Ptolemy identified as Caerbantorigum, one of the main fortresses of the Celtic tribe, the Selgovae. It's thought their territory stretched across the western borders to Nithsdale and it's been suggested that their name, corrupted, survives in the word Solway.

The Selgovae and the Elliots of Liddesdale would have got on swimmingly, albeit in sign language or pidgin Celt. Family loyalties underpinned both their systems. Cattle were a symbol of wealth. From what little we know about the ways of the Celtic tribes and the much fuller record of the exploits of the Elliots, it seems they were both belligerent peoples, easily slighted and unhappy to accept any authority but that of their own hierarchy. Jock Elliot and the boss man of Caerbantorigum could have done business. Mind you, they'd probably have been knocking seven bells out of each other shortly afterwards.

But as we're in romantic mood and struggling take our minds off what's turned into drizzle down the neck, perhaps we should brighten ourselves up by indulging in a bit of Border balladry as we stride out towards Scotch Kershope.

O have ye na heard o' the fause Sakelde?
O have ye na heard o' the keen lord Scroope?
How they hae ta'en bauld Kinmont Willie
On Haribee to hang him up?

The ballad of Kinmont Willie is probably the most famous bit of propaganda to come out of the Borders. The incident it commemorates certainly ended with the best known of all the Border raids. As George Fraser puts it in *The Steel Bonnets*, it was 'a cold-war episode which was to cause diplomatic activity in both capitals'.

It all began at a day of truce held at Kershopefoot on 17 March 1596. It was a routine meeting to sort out petty cross-border misdemeanours. It wasn't even significant enough for the high heid yins to attend. England sent Salkeld, the Deputy Warden, and Scotland's man was Scott of Haining, the Deputy Keeper of Liddesdale. One of his party was William Armstrong of Kinmont, who operated his rackets from a tower at Morton Rigg right on the Border by the western end of the Scots Dike. Trouble was Kinmont Willie's shadow. He'd been in the first division of most-wanted reivers for more than a decade.

There may well have been some sort of row and, if there was, Armstrong would most surely have been in the thick of it. But the meeting apparently ended peacefully enough and the various participants headed for home. As we've seen, the law of the Marches gave them all a sort of diplomatic immunity until sunrise the following day. Armstrong rode off along the Scottish west bank of the Liddel towards Canonbie and Morton Rigg, and the substantial English contingent – upwards of two hundred riders – set off along the east bank in the same direction, heading for Carlisle.

But at some point either Armstrong shouted one insult too many across the water or simply the sight of a known villain riding free got to be too much for Deputy Warden Salkeld and he led his men across the river in pursuit. After a long chase Armstrong of Kinmont was taken prisoner and tied to his horse in the way outlaws were brought home by the sheriff's posse to Laramie. He was paraded through the Sands at Carlisle and imprisoned in the castle.

At which point the 'normal diplomatic channels' became increasingly undiplomatic. The Scots claimed that the Border code that underpinned activities such as the days of truce had been violated. They put it about that the English planned to hang Armstrong on Gallows Hill at Harraby south of Carlisle. In fact he wasn't even in the cells. He was being kept on a sort of parole in one of the houses in the castle's outer ward. The English Warden, Lord Scrope, who arrived back from a spot of leave to find himself in the middle of this diplomatic incident, tried to claim that Armstrong had infringed the rules of the truce day in some unspecified way and so the arrest was justified. Claim and counterclaim were batted back and forth across the Border and as far as Queen Elizabeth's private office. Old scores and grievances fuelled the exchanges.

But eventually the other, more robust, Border law kicked in. Scott of Buccleuch, Keeper of Liddesdale, was tired of being palmed off with English excuses and put out a contract. It was stitched up at a race meeting at Langholm. The Scotts and their neighbours would put up the manpower, various disaffected English officers were bought and some of the staff at Carlisle Castle were bribed. On Sunday 13 April 1596 a small group of riders headed for Carlisle at dead of night. They rode down Stanwix Bank and into the city, found the back door of the castle conveniently open, lifted the prisoner and rode home. Kinmont Willie had his feet up in the tower at Morton Rigg before daybreak.

It was the worst embarrassment of Lord Scrope of Bolton's long career as a warden. He didn't lose his job, but there was much sniggering behind hands. The Bold Buccleuch eventually made a sort of peace with Queen Elizabeth, travelling to London to kiss her hand. The story goes that she asked him how he dared break into her castle of Carlisle, to which he said something like, 'What is there that a man will not dare?' Very Douglas Fairbanks, and prompting the Queen to comment that with ten thousand such men King James of Scotland could shake any throne in Europe. Roll end credits.

Kinmont Willie, meanwhile, continued his reiving, passed on the skills to his four sons and, most likely, died in his bed at Morton Rigg at about the same time that James VI was acceding to the English throne.

One day, not so many years ago, one of the leading lights of the Clan Armstrong Trust took me to meet Kinmont Willie. The tower of Sark churchyard is just across the road from the site of the tower at Morton Rigg. They've been burying Armstrongs and Johnstones here since the sixteenth century.

On many of their gravestones and grave slabs is a skull and crossbones, remembering not an earlier age of Border piracy but the minimum kit of body parts that the Archangel would need on the Day of Resurrection. My guide peeled back a sod and revealed a gloriously well-preserved grave slab. Into it was carved the saltire and from it rose the strong arm brandishing a sword. This, he believed, was the last resting place of the man captured in *The Steel Bonnets* as 'The old robber, full of years and dishonour'. No skull and crossbones here. Presumably old Armstrong of Kinmont had abandoned hope of rising into a golden dawn. But there was the saltire. After years of vacillation and disloyalty, at his last breath he'd declared himself for Scotland.

In his summing up of the Kinmont Willie story George Fraser writes what I think is probably the fairest epitaph for the reivers that I've come across.

The Kinmont raid was a small affair, in itself, but it remains the brightest of Border legends . . . If it was less romantic than the popular legend suggests, it is still a little gem within the strictly professional limits of guerrilla warfare or international crime, depending on how it is viewed. Its importance is less what it was, than what people think it was; if it casts a better, more chivalrous light on the Border reivers than they generally deserved, it still shows them at their best. When men put their lives in the hazard for a single friend, with no thought of gain and only the spice of mischief to set against the risk of death, it is not altogether unworthy.

In an age of counsellors and consultants and political correctness, of ambulance-chasing solicitors and the blame culture, you may disagree. But if you do, you shouldn't have bought this book.

CHAPTER SIX

Scotch Kershope

Two houses guard the approaches to the upper Kershope Valley. In clearings in the trees English and Scots Kershope face each other across the burn. They suffer hardly at all from passing trade. Beyond them I find myself on the wrong bank and have to paddle across to the English side to get to Kershope Head. It was a shepherd's cottage in Logan Mack's day. Now it's run by the Mountain Bothies Association as a billet for lonely walkers. The first greeting inside the door is a sign which says TOILET SPADE and instructions about how to find a good source of water a short walk away in the forest – hopefully in the opposite direction from where the spade has been used.

But these are modern conveniences. The two young surveyors, John Johnson and John Goodwyn would have had to rough it at Kershope Head when they came here at the beginning of the seventeenth century. They were preparing *A Book of the Survaie of the Debateable and Border Lands belonginge to the Crowne of England lyinge betwixt the West and East seas and aboundinge upon the Realm of Scotland: taken in the yeare of our Lorde God 1604*. It was the most comprehensive survey of the Border that had ever been undertaken. Its aim was to maximize the revenues from King James's newly acquired English Borderlands. 351,130 acres were surveyed, 1,143 tenants recorded. Johnson and Goodwyn estimated that the revenue from annual rents could rise from £302 13s. 6d. to £5,074 12s. 4d. Understandably King James was delighted, and on top of the £372 he'd paid them for the job he ordered that they be given a royal bonus of £251 for 'their paynes and traveile therin'.

Their paynes and traveile tidied up many of the Border anomalies that had been allowed to fester during the sixteenth century. With both crowns on the same head nothing was to be gained by squabbling over the odd mile or two of ground. Tenants could no longer use Border disputes as a way of getting out of paying their rent. The old Border of Scottish claim, four miles south-east of Kershope Head on Christianbury Crag, was finally abandoned.

Not that the reiving stopped immediately in King James's Middle Shires. The story's told that when James VI went to live in his English capital in 1603, he took with him his favourite dun cow, which was put out to pasture in the Great Park at Windsor. But the old girl couldn't settle in the soft south and made a break for freedom. Some weeks later she turned up in her old field outside Edinburgh. The King was less amazed by her long journey and navigation skills than by the fact she'd got across the Border without being lifted by an Armstrong or a Graham.

If Lady Daisy of Holyrood could make it from London to Edinburgh, we should be able to make it to Christianbury Crag. But the diversion needs serious contemplation. It's at that point on the sliding scale of walking difficulty where SAS training meets ingrained masochism. So I won't trouble you with descriptions of blundering through the forest. You don't need to know about the acres of grasping, tripping heather. I'll spare you accounts of legs and other bits disappearing into hidden, boggy runnels. I won't go for the sympathy vote. Instead I'll let the book do what the book does best – transport you to that point on the hill where, just ahead of you, is the towering fortress of Christianbury: weathered, shattered rocks soaring out of that part of the Bewcastle Fells that was once Scotland. The boulders are pockmarked by circular holes worn away by wind and rain. And in the frost-riven cracks between the blocks of stone are deposits of a fine, sharp sand which Logan Mack said was much in demand in the 1920s by farmers who used it to sharpen their scythes. The last bit of the climb through drifts of cloudberries is a delight, with its promise of wide views over the trees to the shimmering Solway and to the south-west the receding greys of the Lake District mountains. Behind Christianbury is one of the bleakest views in Britain, which in 1754 Emanuel Bowen, Geographer to George II, described on his map as 'Mountainous and desart parts, uninhabited. A large wast.' It hasn't changed a lot.

But when you've made it to the top, the best view of all is below you. Stretching lance-straight to the south-west for a mile and a half through a ride in the forest and pointing directly at the distant Solway is the great trench known as the Fosse of the Galwegians. It's up to fifteen feet wide and three deep. It would have been much deeper before the peat crept back. Who dug it no one knows for certain. It could have been the Selgovae of south-west Scotland, although a tribe called the Novantae would, more accurately, be described as the people of Galloway. If it was one of those Celtic peoples, the trench would have been a tribal frontier adopted later as the Border – just because it was there. But it could have been created many centuries after the Celtic tribes had been bottled up in Wales, set out by medieval bureaucrats as a marker to tidy up the disputed Border line. Whatever the origins of the trench, John Speede, in his atlas printed in 1610, *The Theatre of the Empire of Great Britain,* shows the Border on Christianbury. But this line in the peat is now an historical punctuation mark, abandoned on a scarcely read page of a remote landscape.

Sitting there at Christianbury as the cloud breaks for a while, revealing distant views altogether too good to hurry, I decide I am going to change my name by deed poll. For the rest of this walk I've decided to be Archibald the Grim. I think it suits me. In case you're thinking that my final, lonely marble has rolled away into the cloudberry, maybe I should explain that it is a perfectly logical thought process. Fosse of the Galwegians > Galloway > Lord of Galloway > Archibald the Grim.

In the fourteenth century Archibald, the 3rd Earl of Douglas, was some baby. His influence spread far beyond his own little corner of south-west Scotland. His anti-English credentials were impeccable and his misdeeds were legendary. He'd fought against the English in France and he was a bellicose Lord Warden of the Scottish West March. At the end of the 1360s, when Annandale as far north as Lochmaben, Roxburghshire to beyond Hawick and most of Berwickshire were in English hands, Archibald began the process of undermining English authority and nibbling the Border back to a line close to the one we recognize today.

He also elbowed his way into folklore. It's said he was a giant of a man who would think nothing of strangling opponents with his bare hands. His island castle at Threave had particularly big corbels to facilitate the hanging of his enemies. It must have looked a picture as guests turned up for the odd dinner party to find the castle festooned with corpses in rather the same way that we drape twinkly icicles round the eaves at Christmas time. He also proved that it wasn't just the plate-handed common reivers who had all the good names. 'Grrrim by name. Grrrim by nature.' And a deep, wild laugh echoed across the forest.

From the summit of Christianbury you can look out to a line of lesser rock outcrops that stretch south to the Long Bar. From a face on this escarpment in the seventh century the stone was quarried to create the Bewcastle Cross, the finest Anglian cross in Britain. Its runic inscriptions commemorate the life and pray for the resurrection of Alcfrith, son of Oswy and King of Northumbria. But to get the fifteen-foot pillar of stone to the unknown craftsman who carved its elaborate

Christian symbols, it had to be manhandled for four and a half miles through the peat hags of the Whitelyne Common.

When Logan Mack walked out to the Long Bar, he found the little quarry. And he found what he believed was a second Bewcastle stone. It was fractured where the Anglo-Saxon quarrymen had tried to ease it from the bedrock. Beside it was a space from which the Bewcastle Cross itself could have come. So could it have been that the original plan was to set a cross at the head and at the foot of the grave of Bewcastle's Anglo-Saxon king? Or was the second stone cut because the first had broken? Discuss. As we head back to the valley of the Kershope Burn.

We're in the Middle March, which runs from Kershope to Cheviot and which was credited with having forty-four 'passages and byeways for the theafe'. One of the busiest was the remote crossing of the Lamisik Foord, as it's described in the Johnson and Goodwyn Survey of 1604. By now the Kershope Burn is just a trickle through forestry that has grown up and, in some areas, even been harvested and replanted since Logan Mack's visit in the 1920s. This is a spot where two countries and three counties meet – the March of Roxburghshire, Northumberland and Cumberland. The author posed for a photograph here, standing plus-foured by a broken wall in Scotland with another member of the party leaning on a Northumberland fencepost and his collie dog lying in Cumberland. It's the loneliest of places. It would have been a perfect gathering spot for people engaged in black work. The old way of Roxburgh is a long way from prying eyes.

But not from the sign builders of the Forestry Commission. On a grassy knoll by the Kershope Burn they've put up not one but three boundary markers turned in towards each other like exhibits at some sign-writers' convention. They mark the place where three forestry conservancies meet – the Newcastleton forest in the south of Scotland and the north-east and north-west conservancies of Kielder and Kershope in England. As there's scarcely a blade of grass out of place around them, it's probably safe to conclude that these signs are, as yet, untroubled by mass tourism.

So you have to wonder about the high-level meeting of officers of the Forestry Commission at which it was decided that signs at Lamisik Ford were essential. Were all three conservancies involved in the decision-making process? Were specialist consultants employed? Was each sign paid for out of a separate regional, if not national, budget? Had any of the people involved ever been here? Will anybody ever come here again? As I wandered away up a burn that was shrinking into a gutter and then a drain and then a damp patch, I had the feeling that the signs had been put up especially for me and that I'd probably be the last person to see them.

CHAPTER SEVEN

The Skyspace building

Whoever Hobb was, his flow is hellish.

Hobb's Flow beyond the Lamisik Ford is a desolate mire in this weather and I suspect it's not a great deal better in high summer. Out of its acres of smelly sponge flows, or rather seeps, Clark's Sike, which becomes the Kershope Burn. It's a bog trapped behind the Larriston Fells. It's so wet that even the tree planters have left it alone. It's a bloody silly place to put the Border.

For the first time since the Scots Dike the Border abandons natural features in the landscape and cuts a straight dash due north for a couple of miles as if trying to get through the mire as quickly as possible. Apparently there used to be an earth embankment that marked the line across the Flow, but that's long since washed away. Of the line of posts that replaced it only stumps are left. I suspected my legs were going the same way so, like Logan Mack when he came this way, I headed for the higher and drier ground.

Grouse rose, clattering and grumbling, but none of them old enough to remember the last human being to venture here. There are cairns and crooked stones in the distance – the Grey Lads – and beyond them the slope of the hill falls away to Larriston itself. The local big shot, Elliot of Larriston, was celebrated by the Ettrick shepherd poet, James Hogg, in 1797 in his tale of the sixteenth-century Borderland.

Lock the door, Larriston, Lion of Liddesdale;
Lock the door, Larriston, Lowther comes on;
The Armstrongs are flying,
The widows are crying,
The Castleton's burning and Oliver's gone.

Larriston stood on one of the main reiving routes across the Border into Tynedale and in James Hogg's rhythms you can hear the dull thunder of horses across Larriston Fell, as the people of Liddesdale fell back from a reprisal raid on the valley led by Lowther and his English allies:

Bewcastle brandishes high his proud scimitar,
Ridley is riding his fleet-footed grey,
Hedley and Howard there,
Wandale and Windermere,
Lock the door, Larriston, keep them at bay.

Just over fifty years before Hogg wrote his poem, Bonnie Prince Charlie stayed a night at Larriston during his advance through Liddesdale in 1745. If he'd hoped the Elliots would jump into the saddle and follow him, he was sorely disappointed. Their fighting instincts had been curbed by then. But I read somewhere that another visitor to Larriston was the author Bernard Cornwell. He used to spend schoolboy holidays staying at Larriston farm. Maybe his character Sharpe has something of the reivers in him.

In the distance there's a blob. It catches the watery sun against the dark wall of trees that, for two miles, marks the Border. Again, forest in England, open moor in Scotland. Some maps mark the site of a battle near the blob, for no better reason than the name of the place somehow deserves a battle. This is Bloody Bush.

But what happened here was a skirmish rather than a clash of armies (a sanguinary encounter, as James Logan Mack puts it). The story goes that a group of Tynedale raiders, probably Robsons, were daft enough to settle themselves for the night here on the way back from a raid on Liddesdale. The Armstrongs and Elliots found them and cut them down to a man. And they wouldn't have been difficult to find. They'd camped beside the reiving equivalent of the A7. A road from

Dinlabyre in Liddesdale to Lewisburn in Tynedale. A track which started life as a shortcut between two valleys but which eventually became one of the metalled trade routes across the Border. It was a highway for several hundred years but abandoned with the coming of the Border Counties Railway from Riccarton Junction on the Waverley line to Hexham. It's an example of just how quickly nature gets its own back. You can still find patches of tarred surface, but the weeds have eaten most of it away.

The blob is the Bloody Bush toll pillar, set up in the 1830s to mark the boundary between the properties of Sir J.E. Swinburn, Bart, of Capheaton in Northumberland and William Oliver Rutherford of Dinlabyre. Its inscription sets out the scale of charges on their private toll road.

For horses employed in leading coals	2d each
All other horses	3d do.
Cattle	1d do.
Sheep, Calves, Swine	1/2d do.

Coal from the Lewisburn and Plashetts collieries in Tynedale fuelled the clattering woollen mills of Hawick and was carried across this road in the creels of packhorses. Its importance as a commercial thoroughfare is shown by the quality and size of the pillar. James Logan Mack was fascinated by what things weigh, for some reason. Bloody Bush toll was 27 tons by his reckoning, 15 feet high and 6 feet square, of well-cut stone, in what appears to be the middle of nowhere.

But if you come here (and even if you don't), just take a few minutes to look at the map. Everywhere there are overgrown relics of ages when this was a busy landscape. Cairns and quarries, earthworks and settlements. Continuity. Today

Bloody Bush is a forgotten important place. A blustery wind funnelled the rain through a ride in the forest and lashed it against the pillar. I took shelter in the trees and extracted the remains of an egg and tomato sandwich that looked as if it, too, had been through a sanguinary encounter.

For a mile beyond Bloody Bush a broken wall and faint traces of the trenches that mark the Border hug the edge of the trees. But then for no rhyme or reason that's obvious today they suddenly turn to the east and plunge into the middle of the forest. What comes next is six miles of cartographic eccentricity.

Even the seriously well prepared Logan Mack almost got lost here, trying to track the Border across what was then open moor. This is the stretch marked as disputed ground on a map produced as late as 1837. We're luckier because we've got the forest as a handrail. The forest is a great respecter of national frontiers, presumably because the English division of the Forestry Commission doesn't want the Scottish division half inching its trees. Open rides through the forest track the Border across the slopes and almost to the summit of Buckside Knowe. But there must have been another dispute here because the line veers off and then doubles back on itself, leaving the summit in Scottish territory. Then we're heading due north to something shown on the map as the Duke's Well. As the spring is in England, it was presumably the Duke of Northumberland's.

It's also one of the sources of the Bells Burn, and the Border meanders with the peaty stream for a mile and a half past Shielsike Crag in England, the March Sike in Scotland and Anthon's Linn waterfalls in both. Anthon's Linn is probably named after an English outlaw called Anton Armstrong who, in 1541, led Liddesdale in a bloody revolt that burned Bewcastle and helped persuade Henry VIII to abandon diplomacy and let his liver be the arbiter of national policy. The King's advisors tried to persuade him that his jaundiced view of Anglo-Scottish relations was a mistake, but he would hear nothing of it. He backed his hangover and won a great victory at the battle of Solway Moss.

The March Sike may have marked an earlier course of the Border. And the name Shielsike is a reminder of the way that these hills used to be farmed. In summer, shepherds would drive their flocks out on to the high pastures and stay with them, living in shielings on the hill. And it's interesting that this Border version of transhumance took precedence over reiving. The summer months, when flocks had to be tended on the hill and hay had to be gathered in, were a closed season for the reivers. But by the back end of August they were getting twitchy again, looking forward to sharp cold nights under a full moon. And the reiver's wife would be polishing the spur that she would lay on her husband's empty plate one evening to remind him that supplies were running low and it was time to be in the saddle again.[16]

The Border used to continue all the way down the Bells Burn to where it winds into the North Tyne half a mile ahead. But just below an insignificant little waterfall called Bells Linn it goes walkabout again, heading north-west this time and marked by a broken wall that leads towards the shoulder of Thorlieshope Pike. Not for the last time on our stroll we'll find a substantial chunk of England lying due north of Scotland.

Just down the burn from where the Border ratches off across the fell is the site of the Bells Kirk. You can still find the rectangular outline of what remains of its walls, much as

16 The spur that featured in that famous border tale is still owned by the Charlton family at Hesleyside

Logan Mack saw them in the 1920s. Most of the kirk has been recycled into a byre by the burn, which in turn is being recyled by wind and weather into a ruin. But the large block of sandstone, a yard square and hollowed into a bowl, which may well have been the Bells Kirk font, still lies among the sieves. Bells Kirk was probably a chapel of ease served by monks who walked across the hills from the substantial priory at Canonbie. But it was more important politically than ecclesiastically. This was another of the appointed meeting places of the Wardens of the March, like the Lochmabonstone and Kershopefoot. When the Border followed the burn to its mouth, Bells Kirk was just in Scotland. Today it's about a hundred yards into England. A hundred yards of bog and rock that once exercised some of the greatest minds in two countries as they wrangled over points of territorial principle. But it was more than a diplomatic nicety to a hotly pursued Border reiver. To him, those hundred yards were a matter of life or death. Reach the church and ring the bell and he had sanctuary. He couldn't be hauled back across the Border to answer for his crime. At least not if anybody was looking.

And for most of the time no one was. The laws of the Marches were played out in full costume at days of truce. Niceties of legal detail would be argued and tested. Weighty judgements would be handed down. But most of the time the communities of the Border cleaned up their own mess. If a community in Redesdale or Liddesdale had their sheep stolen, they'd go after them. And they wouldn't be consulting the manual of Border etiquette or hanging about for a Border official to turn up with the regulation turf on his lance. When they caught up with the raiders there would be no warning shots, no debate about extenuating circumstances. At the end of it all those who remained alive on each side would take home their dead and wounded. Apart from a few patches of blood in the heather it would be as if the raid and the retribution had never happened. I suspect that the cases which came to court at truce days were the exception rather than the rule and more often than not concerned with the sub-plots of frontier life, the web of family feuding and political point scoring.

The Border wall from Thorlieshope Pike zigzags along what looks like a dried-up stream across Bells Moor. (It was the only dried-up thing that day.) On the way down there's the site of Hawkhope Hole, a village settled by fugitives from the Scottish clearances in the seventeenth century and now vanished apart from a scattering of earthworks. I tramped about a bit looking for them but could find only a sheepfold. A surge of blustery rain out of Liddesdale ensured I didn't look very hard.

But the next aiming mark in the landscape is rather easier to find if, on the face of it, a little difficult to explain. Why they built a railway station at Deadwater is hard to fathom. It must have served all of about six houses. There's no Deadwater Hall whose owner demanded a private halt in return for letting the railway through. There were quarries, but a siding would have been sufficient for them. Yet here it is. A station for ghost trains. An earlier traveller described it as 'A Lilliputian station displaying with laconic pathos on its narrow platform a name embalmed in Border song and story. Who uses it I can't imagine.' [17]

When Logan Mack marched in from the fell he found that, despite appearances, this outpost of the railway empire was, indeed, fully operational. 'This station must be one of the least important in the British Islands, serving as it does so sparsely populated a district. No proper roadway leads to it,

17 A.G. Bradley, *The Romance of Northumberland*, Methuen & Co., 1908

access being obtained by a footpath across a field. It is under the charge of one female official, who is empowered to issue tickets to but six stations.'

When I marched in from the fell the one female official had been replaced by a very pleasant couple who'd bought the station as a holiday home. They were having terrible problems with rabbits undermining the wooden-framed station platform, which they'd turned into a neatly mown lawn. And they weren't empowered to sell tickets to anywhere, the nearest surviving railway being at least thirty miles away. The only through traffic that disturbed their isolation was mountain bikers who'd ride another fifty yards along the line of the track, have their photograph taken by the WELCOME TO SCOTLAND sign thoughtfully provided by the Forestry Commission, and then turn round and ride back into England.

Having taken a few moments to convince the couple's throaty black Labrador that I wasn't the advance party of a reiving raid, I went in search of the district's other industry – tourism.

A more unlikely tourist destination is hard to imagine. Deadwater is a wide, slack expanse of sodden bog. It was identified as 'Ye Red Moss' in the Johnson and Goodwyn survey of 1604. The rivers North Tyne and Liddel both start here by the grassy mire that's known as Deadwater Lakes before turning their backs on each other and heading for opposite coasts. But once, people came from all over the Borders and beyond to take the waters (and there was obviously no shortage of them) at Deadwater Spa. The collapsed remains of the baths that were filled from its mineral spring are in a clearing in the wood beside the line of the railway just as it crosses into Scotland. The flaking and the itching would come here in their hundreds to find cures for their 'cutaneous and scrofulous complaints'. But if you're thinking that they built Deadwater station to serve an influx of scratchers, I'm afraid that theory holds water about as well as the ruins of the bath house. Certainly visitors in great numbers had been making the medicinal pilgrimage to Deadwater since the middle of the eighteenth century, but the spring's popularity had subsided by the time they drove the railway over the hills from Riccarton Junction in the 1860s.

Just a couple of miles along the valley from Deadwater, in the opposite direction from our route of march but worth a visit if your legs are still hanging together, is Kielder. It's hemmed in by the forest now, but it used to be a wild and woolly place. Sir Walter Scott, always up for a free lunch with the aristocracy, used to visit the Duke of Northumberland at the pretend Border castle he built here as a shooting lodge. In his journal for 7 October 1827 Scott reports:

> The Duke tells me his people in Keeldar were all quite wild, the first time his father went up to shoot there. [We're talking somewhere in the late 1750s or early 1760s.] The women had no other dress than a bedgown and petticoat. The men were savage and could hardly be brought to rise from the heath, either from sullenness or fear. They sung a wild tune the burden of which was 'Ourina, Ourina, Ourina'. The females sung, the men danced round and at a certain point in the tune they drew their dirks which they always wore.

These were the poor remnants of the reiving Charltons and Robsons, Milburns and Dodds, a century and a half after prosperity and progress settled on the Border. Quite where they learned to sing the Spanish for 'piss off' is something of a mystery, but at least they hadn't yet sunk to the abject forelock-tugging that marked out later generations' responses to the Dukes of Northumberland. An ancient resident of Kielder once told me that when the great family came here for the shooting in the 1920s local schoolchildren were forced to line the approach to the castle, the boys saluting and the girls curtseying as the ducal cars went by. Their reward was a show of silent cowboy films starring Tom Mix and Tony the Wonder Horse, organized by the Duchess in the castle dining room. Older estate workers – the men had to stop and remove their caps, the women curtsey as the Northumberland family drove by – were treated to a dance on the polished boards of the wooden bridge over the Kielder Burn. Ah, the good old days when people knew their place.

If plans laid in the 1950s had been implemented, Kielder would have become very different. The Northumberlands had handed over the estate in lieu of death duties by then and the only government agency even remotely interested in this tract of poor land on the Border was the Forestry Commission. It planned a New Town complete with shopping mall and curling rink. Five thousand forestry workers and their families would have lived there. But then they realized they could maintain the biggest man-made forest in Britain with contract labour who could find their own place to live, and plans for Kielder New Town were abandoned. The few rows of forestry houses that were built have been voted the most remote village in England – and one of the most pleasant places to live. Just so long as you're not a compulsive shopper or curling fan.

I met Bernie McFadden at Kielder. He used to be a copper in Whitley Bay, so had first-hand knowledge of wildlife. Even so, his new job as ranger at the Kielder visitor centre must have come as a bit of a shock to the system. Bernie had obviously not been a 'stitch 'em up, hang 'em high' sort of copper. It was hard to imagine him wading into the disorderly drunks outside Spanish City of a Saturday night. He has a natural gentleness about him and the Forestry Commission would have been hard pressed to find a more enthusiastic spokesman for the delights of Kielder. He took me on the grand tour – goshawks here, deer in the clearing over there, a wonderful skewed railway viaduct abandoned in the forest and enough species of plant to make Linnaeus rise from the dead.

And, as the dusky afternoon closed in on us, in the attics of Kielder Castle, we climbed about in a cobwebbed jumble of forest history. Pictures tracing the development of 'the great venture' that was the Kielder Forest, the draining, ploughing and planting of the moorland, Land Army girls dressed in skimpy suntops and moleskin shorts lined up on a fallen tree, posing and smiling for the camera sometime in the 1940s. They're probably grandmothers now and telling their granddaughters that they really ought to wear something less revealing when they go nightclubbing. In another box there were later pictures of the flooding of the valleys to make the Kielder reservoir and faded photographs of farms that survived centuries of Border raiding and warfare but succumbed to the bulldozers pushing history to one side as they scooped out the biggest man-made lake in Europe.

Most of the photographs were taken by a remarkable survivor. Valdemars Blankenburg was the chief inspector of engineers for the Latvian Forest Service at the outbreak of the Second World War. With his young wife and baby son he went on the run, from first the Germans and then the Russians. Eventually from the Americans, too, who were planning to hand Latvians back to the Russians. In one year alone 34,000 Latvians were deported to the Soviet Union and disappeared without trace. But the Blankenburgs knew the forest and it hid them until they could make contact with

British troops. Having made it to Britain, at Kielder they found another forest haven where Valdemars stayed for the rest of his life, taking more than 15,000 photographs of the works in progress. As the forest surveyor he reckoned he'd walked 12,000 miles back and forth across the Kielder moorland. He probably knew the lie of the land even better than the Liddesdale Armstrongs.

In the early evening Bernie and I drove up into high Kielder along some of the seven hundred miles of extraction roads that quarter the forest. On a hill overlooking the reservoir we sat for a while in Skyspace, a circular building with a circular hole in its white dome, through which we watched a disc of scudding clouds as the sky turned first mauve and then imperial purple. Silly thought, I know, but what would Banepryke have made of it if he'd stumbled across a bit of installation art on his way back from a raid on Plashetts? It would have comfortably held eight or ten black cattle while the old villain took a breather and his dogs snarled and bayed at the moon.

CHAPTER EIGHT

The Reideswire Stone

B ack at Deadwater the next train from platform one will be never. So we'd better walk. Starting from the north end of Deadwater station, the line of the abandoned railway is the Border for a few hundred yards until the route turns east again across Deadwater Rigg, hugging the edge of the Myredykes plantation. It's the start of a wearisome slog up the 1,975 feet of Peel Fell.

Before you start the climb, look up to the western shoulder of Deadwater Fell, where you can pick out a huge windworn rock called the Boar Stone. Striated and shattered, it has a four-foot-square tunnel carved through the middle of it by frost and wind and water. Get the angle just right and you can see the sky through it. Which puts off the attempt on Peel Fell for another few minutes.

Golden rule of long walks uphill number one: always arm yourself with an array of excuses to disguise the fact you've stopped to get your breath back. This of course matters only if you're walking in company.

As I'm walking in yours, I've stopped just before being hemmed in by the trees that blanket the lower slopes – not, of course, to get my breath back but because I'm crossing what appears on the map as the line of an ancient track called the Wheel Causeway. There are faint traces of a roadway bounded by shallow ditches, so faint that they could be nothing more than sunken field drains to which have been added a dollop of imagination. Some claim the road is Roman, and that it got its name from the fact it was once the only road suitable for wheeled traffic in this remote district. Which sounds a bit obvious. Others say that Wheel has been corrupted from quheil, meaning the place where water from a spring collects, and that Causeway is a corruption of the old Northumbrian word causey, which means limestone. Which sounds a bit convoluted. The road has also been referred to as the West Causeway[18] and it's said that it joins up with an ancient tribal boundary dyke on the slopes of Peel Fell. This is the Catrail, which supposedly ran south from Galashiels and continued as the Northumbrian Black Dyke, both raised as defensive works against Agricola's invasion of the north. Of the Catrail I could find no trace, but I bet somebody will write to tell me how easy it is to find if you're not concentrating on getting your breath back.

Where the Wheel Causeway/Quheil Causey/ West Causeway crosses Wheel Rigg a mile or two to the north of us there was another medieval village and yet another church, the Wheel Kirk, both now lost in the forest. After the sacking of Berwick in 1296, during which many thousands of people were slaughtered in what's been described as an act of terrorism by the army of Edward I, the King spent a night at the Wheel Kirk on his way to do penance at the shrine of St Ninian in Galloway. Ninian, the founding father of Scottish Christianity, was obviously unimpressed by his royal visitor. The following year Berwick was avenged and the English army cut to pieces by the forces of William Wallace at the battle of Stirling Bridge.[19]

Breath back. Move on. Heading for the twin cairns that top off Peel Fell. The Border runs between them. And this is where the landscape shakes itself free of habitation. Ahead of us

18 Brigadier General William Sitwell, *The Border from a Soldier's Point of View*, Andrew Reid and Co., Newcastle, 1927
19 I found the reference to Edward I's visit to the Wheel Kirk in a wonderful little book called *No Road this Way after Dark*, Geordie Harkness's reminiscences of Liddesdale. It's a gem of first-hand local history, available from the Heritage Centre in Newcastleton.

we've got the best part of forty miles of high, lonely country. Apart from our trips off the hill to find a bed for the night, the nearest we'll get to civilization is the bacon butty van in the lay-by at the Carter Bar. And just to cheer you up that's only about six miles away.

I've been to the top of Peel Fell before. To be more precise I've been round the top of it two or three times at about seventy-five feet in an over-engined biscuit tin. We were filming the *Walking the Line* series and were trying to find somewhere to land near the Kielder Stone. I should explain that I have had a certain antipathy to helicopters ever since I was told that pilots in the Vietnam war used to describe the single fitting that holds the rotors on as the Jesus nut. But that's by the by. The fact is that helicopters are not all they're cracked up to be. On that aerial reconnaissance we'd quartered the ground, getting a bird's eye view of a bleak expanse of moor littered with stones that all looked remarkably similar. Over the crackling intercom we debated which of them was the Kielder Stone.

On the ground there's no mistaking it. The descent along the Border follows a raggedy burn from Peel Fell. Then the ground dips away more steeply and there it is below you. A block of flats in the heather. As you get lower and closer, its sheared edge starts to look like the prow of a ship becalmed in a green-brown rolling sea. If any natural feature deserves, by its sheer presence, to be the mark of the Border, this is it. But until the 1770s this was disputed ground. For sixteen years Hugh, Earl and later Duke of Northumberland, and Archibald Douglas of Douglas in the Shire of Lanark had argued about which of them owned this tract of back of beyond. Nasty letters passed back and forth between the estate owners. Surveys were conducted on an agreed scale of eight chains to the inch, which discovered what any local could have told them for free:

'It is one Continued Flow almost impassable and very little value.'

The bickering over the Keilder Stone and its surrounding peat bogs was just the final chapter in a long and dishonourable feud that started in the 1330s between Henry Percy, the Northumberlands' ancestor, and William, Earl of Douglas. Both were March Wardens responsible for keeping order, but neither saw any conflict of interest between their day job and an increasingly violent disagreement over which of them owned large tracts of land in Roxburghshire. The feud destabilized the Border to such an extent that Edward III sent in armed peacekeepers and eventually ordered the setting up of a commission to sort it out.

Four hundred and forty years later a couple of firms of provincial lawyers managed what all the King's horses and all the King's men had failed to achieve. On 11 May 1778 a settlement was reached by arbitration, which set the estate boundaries and in effect fixed the Border from Peel Fell to Carter Fell.[20] From that date the Border indisputably ran through the middle of the Kielder Stone.

Logan Mack was much taken by this chunk of fell sandstone. As usual he had his tape measure and scales out: 133 feet in circumference, 26 feet high and weighing 1,400 tons was his estimate. The author and his companions posed for photographs on its ledges. One of the party managed to climb to the top and, more importantly, managed to get down again, unlike a party of local teenagers who were marooned on the rock for a while shortly before Logan Mack's visit. A ladder had to be brought from Deadwater to rescue them. No doubt the parent who carried it over Peel Fell on his shoulder welcomed his

20 I am indebted to Robin Plackett of Newcastle for this information, gleaned from the Duke of Northumberland's archives at Alnwick Castle.

children back to earth with a cheery hug and a peck on the cheek.

Howard Pease in *The Lord Wardens of the Marches* describes it as 'the Mighty Kielder Stone where the Western Wardens met'. They probably did during their routine clean-up operations, but not for formal days of truce. And the reivers would meet here, too. It's inconceivable that this monster on the moor wouldn't have been used as an aiming mark. An assembly point on the way to terrorize the locals in Tynedale or a spot to rendezvous and divide the spoils on the way back. It was, and is, a powerful place. And as such it attracted myth and legend. The grooves in the rock, worked by wind and weather, were reported by occasional nervous visitors to have been seen running with blood – further proof of my long-held suspicion that early travellers who, reportedly, made such light work of long journeys through these hills on foot were invariably drunk.

It was held to be unlucky to ride three times round the Kielder Stone 'withershins' – that's in the opposite direction to the course of the sun. Maybe I'm an insensitive soul but when I was there it seemed perfectly benign. But I was sober, didn't have the hot trod on my tail and was careful to wander round it in the same direction as the sun. If there had been any. Which there wasn't.

The Border line heads north up a steep, knee-wrenching climb through deep and tangled heather. There's a scramble through the gully of Kielderstone Cleuch before the gentler stroll out on to Wylies Craigs with its wide views south over the forest. There will be plenty of those in the next couple of days as we stroll across the roof of the Border. All the way trying to spot the most distant identifiable summits, English and Scots, and looking out for the Logan Mack moments, the occasional places where, if the cloud lifts and the hazes clear, you can see both coasts of Britain.

Ahead, the Border line itself is occasionally marked by boundary stones erected sometime after the 1778 arbitration. There are lots of them, which presumably demonstrates how seriously the Northumberlands and Douglases took their disagreement. Each stone is marked with an N on the English side and a back-to-front D on the Scots. Logan Mack suggests that the ill-educated stonemason who did the job must have been given a stencil for the letters and simply got the D the wrong way round. But a man I met in a pub in Alnwick – and therefore every bit as reliable a witness – told me that by the terms of the arbitration the Duke of Northumberland had to pay to have the stones erected and the back-to-front Ds were a final snook cocked in the direction of the troublesome Douglases.

Many of the events of the Border struggle are concerned with such parish-pump slights and rivalries. It's tempting to write them off as mere twitches of the net curtains of local history. But while the locals understood it was all part of the cut and thrust of frontier life, the Border and its stories and legends had a powerful grip on the imagination of people a very long way from Kielder. The goings on here were known about nationally and internationally.

From the very earliest Border laws – the Leges Marchiarum set out in 1249 – there was provision to recruit manpower from far afield to subdue or defend this troublesome region: 'all men between Totnais [Totnes] in England and Caithness in Scotland can rightly – according to the customs of the said realms – be called to the Marches for combat, with the exception of the persons of the Kings of the said realms and of the Bishops of St. Andrews and Dunkeld.'

In the fifteenth century, during the reign of Edward IV, truces, abstinences from war and Border laws were to be proclaimed over a wide area. In one case announcements were read in thirty-three counties, towns and cities from Northumberland to Calais.[21] The happenings on the Border were hot gossip. Characters like the Bold Buccleuch, particularly after the Kinmont Willie raid, were the soap-opera stars of their day, heroes or villains depending on where the message was being received.

And these events were taking place in the fearsome, alien north. Not a real place but a foreign land that festered in the southern imagination.

This frightening north was a cultural construct, a state of mind. The north of England was always a vague location for those who lived in and around London and the court. Chaucer's two Cambridge students in the Reeve's Tale were northerners who spoke with northern accents, swore by St. Cuthbert and were born in 'Strother', 'far in the north, I cannot tell you where'. Chaucer seems to have been familiar with northerners, but for his audience there was no need to be specific about somewhere so distant. In literary convention the north was somewhere largely unknown, a long way away when one travelled with one's back to the sun.[22]

Even the Bible reinforced the stereotype. There's the line in Jeremiah: 'Out of the north an evil shall break forth upon all inhabitants of the land.'

But set alongside the fears of this alien place were contradictory images of freedom and adventure. The north was a place where ordinary men resisted overweening authority and created their own justice. Outlaws like Adam Bell, the

21 Howard Pease, *The Lord Wardens of the Marches of England and Scotland*, Constable, 1913, limited edition
22 A.J. Pollard, *The Characteristics of the Fifteenth-century North*, Sutton, 1997

Cumbrian Robin Hood, who stole the King's deer in Inglewood forest in Cumberland and ran rings round the Sheriff of Carlisle. For a while the Bold Buccleuch joined this cast list of free-spirited heroes. The problem was that people in the south and even people at court, the officers of state responsible for making policy in the distant Borders, began to believe the myths and legends. The Border became a fairytale frontier.

So it's appropriate that we are heading into a fairy glen. The line of the Border drops away to the junction of two mountain streams, the Green and Black Needles. It's the Black we're going to follow through a narrow and picturesque gorge that twists and wanders through the rising moor. But if the water's running hard, you'll have to find yourself a detour because the banks are so steep you'll have to pick your way along the bottom of the burn. Either that or you could wear chest waders. We pass another tiny burn on our right, sweetly called the Trouting, and then by the remains of a cairn at the next washed-out gully turn towards the high ground.

The next bit is optional.

I hadn't planned to go to Carlin Tooth, because it involves a detour of more than a mile and a half to the north, away from the Border, but that morning I'd had a fax from Logan Mack's granddaughter in Australia and I had a bit of apologizing to do. James Logan Mack loved Carlin Tooth, with its sheared escarpment running out to Hartshorn Pike. He thought it provided one of the best viewpoints on the whole walk. A thousand feet below us the Jed Water rises in a muddy puddle at the start of its journey by way of Teviot to Tweed. Over the trees you can see the length of Liddesdale and, beyond, the shimmer of the Solway washing the feet of the hills of south-west Scotland. To the south the Lakeland mountains are sharp cut under high cloud and to the east there's the route we're about to take across the high Cheviots, leading out to the hill of the goat, Yeavering Bell. That's only fifteen miles or so from the sea, so on a really clear day this should be one of the coast-to-coast moments. You ought to be able to see both sea-washed edges of the Border country from Carlin Tooth. I couldn't, and James Logan Mack couldn't on his visit, but you might have better luck.

But here on Mr Mack's favourite viewpoint, the apology. I've portrayed him as a rather dour and humourless man. And I put it down to his being not just a lawyer but an Edinburgh lawyer at that. So he was obviously pompous, humourless and probably Dickensian mean as well. In fact James Logan Mack was dealt a pretty rotten hand of cards.

It all started comfortably enough. His father was a successful advocate with a town house in Edinburgh and a country estate in Berwickshire. But Logan Mack's mother believed that spared rods spoiled children and he grew up resenting her regular thrashings. As a child he was sensitive and musically gifted. He played the violin but, in childhood, damaged a hand in a bicycle accident and had to give up playing. When he had a family of his own his son, James Victor, died of whooping cough at the age of eighteen months. And just as he was settling into the family law business he discovered that his father had got himself into bad financial trouble, from which the firm never really recovered. Unsurprisingly, he suffered from bouts of depression. Expeditions like the one along the Border Line were an escape. So if his writing about the trip is a touch undemonstrative, who cares? Sorry Mr Mack. Enjoy the view. And look on the bright side. You said that you never wanted to do the next bit of the walk again. And you don't have to.

It's a trudge back to the Border, which runs between two cairns on Duntae Edge, and then you set your face to the north-east for a long squelch through the peat hags of Knocks Knowe and Carter Fell, with Border stones charting the way (and at least giving you somewhere reasonably dry to set your backside), until you start the long drop in to the main road at the Carter Bar, one of the three trunk routes across the Border into Scotland – the new road to Edinburgh by Jedburgh as it was described on a map of 1801. And with sore feet and dampness in every crevice it's my turn to try looking on the bright side. After all, we only have to plod across this high, wet desert to Catcleuch Shin once. People used to have to do a lifetime's work up here. Just before the descent are the remains of coal mines. There are packhorse trails through the heather. And the industrial history is all there to be discovered on the map. To the south of us there's Limestone Knowe. A mile to the north is the Limekiln Burn. The coal was used to fire the kilns that took raw limestone rock and turned it into agricultural lime, a magical potion for farmers in these acidic uplands.

Like tea on a drizzly day. The caravan at the Carter Bar can provide it, and with musical accompaniment. This spot on the A68 is the first glimpse of Scotland for many visitors and I hate to think what effect it has on their view of the country. A couple of competing pipers, one playing 'Scotland the Brave' and the other droning something unidentifiable. Both taking tips from coach parties in their respective lay-bys while trying to outdo the roar of the heavy lorries. The whole cultural experience steeped in a wafting smell of hot dogs and chip fat. And people say the *Braveheart* film distorted Scottish history.

As I sat sipping my styrofoam tea, straining it through the lorry fumes, I found myself wondering which piper was making the most money. The one introducing his expectant audience to the brochure delights of the Scotland to come, or the one who was confirming what returning coach parties already knew: that a once-proud nation now sells itself as a tarty blend of Balmorality and porridge kitsch that would make Mel Gibson blush. Billy Connolly, where art thou at this moment when we need you to take the piss out of the lot of them?

There used to be a lively alehouse here on the Scottish side of the Carter Bar, where *Bravemouth* would have gone down a storm, but the mistress progress put a stop to that. Probably because they didn't have a valid entertainments licence endorsed by the local authority. But I bet the pipers had to work harder for their tips in the Carter Bar. And the neighbours rarely complained about the noise, given that the nearest neighbour would have been several miles away.

In the lay-by I chatted to a quiet American couple from Utah who were on their way to visit Edinburgh before making a pilgrimage to Dumfriesshire. The light of adventure was in their eyes. They'd been planning to 'come home' for more than twenty years but jobs and children and Federal taxes and 11 September had all got in the way. They turned out to be Maxwells whose ancestors had shipped out from Annan Waterfoot during one or other of the Border depressions at the beginning of the nineteenth century. Their Maxwell ancestor had been a cattle drover taking beasts from south-west Scotland to the cattle fairs at Malham and even as far as St Faith's at Norwich. When he emigrated, he easily found work as a cowpoke on the long-distance cattle drives of the American West. Having made a bit of money, he rather carelessly mislaid his Scottish wife and family, took up with a lady from a one-horse town in Utah, and settled down to farming and breeding. The family were still on the same farm.

'She weren't no lady but she was very beautiful.' It was Mrs Utah's first contribution. 'She was a saloon singer, so they say . . .', leaving no room for doubt that they'd obviously said much worse.

'Arch Max-well was a bit of a hell-raiser them days but least she settled him down.' The husband seemed intent on salvaging the beauty's reputation. 'And she was a good mother to twelve children and their eldest boy was my great-great-grandfather.'

I said the Maxwells had always had a reputation for hellraising so Arch was just running true to form, and that he probably thought Wild West Utah was home from home. We talked about the bloody feud between the Maxwells and the Johnstones in the Scottish West March, which George Fraser reckoned was the bitterest family quarrel in British history. In just a few weeks in the mid-1580s the Maxwells and their allies burned eighty Johnstone houses and several villages and hanged anyone who got in their way. Maxwell lords were regularly outlawed and imprisoned, and they had a decidedly portable sense of national loyalty. With each black mark against his family's reputation the husband's smile broadened.

Mrs Utah seemed to feel more comfortable with Maxwell heritage than with their visceral history and said she was most looking forward to seeing their 'wonderful home' at Caerlaverock. I didn't want to dent the anticipation by telling her that her family castle is a touch draughty ever since, in September 1640, besieging anti-royalist forces (the royal in question being Charles I) pulled down enough of it to make sure the place could never be used as a fortress or even a residence again.

But the fairytale castle of her imagination was a real mirror of Border history. Commanding a bridgehead in the marshes on the north shore of the Solway at a time when transport by water could be marginally easier than a route march overland, it was probably built by the English in the closing years of the twelfth century but soon fell into Scottish hands. We know that because Edward I besieged it in 1300. By 1312 the Maxwells had a grip of it. And in a way they never left. By marriage and descent they passed it to the Herries family and then the Dukes of Norfolk, who gave it to the nation in 1946. But in the intervening years this Maxwell blockhouse on the Solway shore became an (almost) invincible triangular fortress and then, as more peaceful times took hold, a grand, renaissance residence fit for a family who'd weathered the storm.

'It sounds very ro-mantic but . . .' said she.

But as we know romance is a dangerous charlatan and, anyhow, whatever she said next was drowned out by the marauding piper.

The drones drifted after me across the fell, but they were soon overtaken by the more musically adept dull roar of traffic. A blessed silence had descended by the time I arrived at the Reideswire Stone, a chunk of rock fenced off from scratching cattle in the middle of the moor. Some say that this was the last place where Englishmen and Scotsmen fought each other as national enemies. In some accounts it's portrayed as a great battle – the spark for the last Anglo-Scottish war. In fact it was a drunken brawl that got spectacularly out of hand.

It started out as a routine meeting of the wardens on 7 July 1575, the saint's day of Thomas the Martyr. Unfortunately the participants forgot to say their prayers.

Sir John Forster was leading the English contingent. He was the most remarkable of all the Border Wardens. Born somewhere about 1501, he survived the whole of the sixteenth century, staying in post for thirty-five years and dying in his bed in 1602. He made many enemies. A group of them tried to kill him in Bamburgh Castle when he was ninety-six and were only stopped by his redoubtable wife barring his bedroom door. Redoubtable and recent: Isabel Sheppard had been Forster's mistress for many years, but luckily for him he'd been persuaded to make an honest woman of her in his old age. He was also a crook, a Godly Rogue as one biographer described him,[23] who used the wardenry to line his deep pockets. When he got old, he lost his grip on the Middle March and the reivers ran rings round him, but in his heyday, when the English Crown decided to set a thief to catch a thief, he was just the man for the job.

At the head of the Scots was Sir John Carmichael, the Keeper of Liddesdale. He was less fortunate, even though he was widely regarded as the best Border officer of his time. The Bishop of Durham described him as 'the most expert Borderer'. He made it into his fifties but on 16 June 1600, when he was riding from Annan to Langholm, he was chased by a motley gang of Armstrongs, Scotts and Irvines and shot down.

Twenty-five years earlier the pair of them were in the thick of routine Border business. That day at the Reidswire the usual rituals were observed. Complaints were laid and everything was going reasonably smoothly, with the normal finger-pointing and hurled obscenities that were the stock in trade of the courts of Border law. But an English offender called Farnstein apparently hadn't shown up to be held hostage until the goods he'd stolen were returned or paid for. Carmichael sharply demanded that Forster deliver him.

Perhaps Forster, the elder statesman and consummate fixer, objected to the way the young whippersnapper Carmichael spoke to him. After all, he wasn't even a fully rigged warden. Maybe a family feud got out of hand with one derogatory remark too many about this or that Tynedale man's dubious parentage. Maybe it was just the drink talking.

23 M. Meikle, 'A Godly Rogue: the Career of Sir John Forster, an Elizabethan Border Warden', *Northern History 28*, 1992

Whatever the cause, the shooting started. There were Scottish casualties. Forster and Carmichael wheeled about on their horses trying to clear the court, but the English squad saw they had the upper hand and drove the Scots off. But at the bottom of the hill a group of Jedburgh men who were arriving late at the truce day provided reinforcements. In the fray that followed, the English Deputy, Sir George Heron, Keeper of Tynedale and Redesdale, was killed. Forster himself and several other English notables were taken prisoner.

The events were well documented and have crept into the seams of popular history as a great Scottish victory. (Perhaps because they had so few.) But more interesting than the Reideswire Fray itself is how it was sorted out and what that process tells us about the state of Anglo-Scottish relations at a time that is often portrayed as the storm before the lull of the Union of the Crowns. By all accounts the English prisoners were well treated and even compensated for their enforced holiday in Scotland. Even though the English authorities were far from certain about Forster's role in the shenanigans (hardly surprising, given his track record), they demanded that Carmichael was handed over as a pledge, but he was soon back home in Liddesdale. It was all very businesslike and all very gentlemanly.

Bureaucracy was kicking in. It was too early yet to say it was all over bar the shouting. There would be another thirty years of lawlessness and violence. In fact, some of the worst reiving trouble in the long history of Border conflict would take place in the final straight. But the machinery of government was grinding, ever so slowly, towards a new order. A brave new world in which, if the new King of England had his way, the Border would become irrelevant.

CHAPTER NINE

Remains of Roman camps at Chew Green

t the same time as the Reideswire Fray was being sorted out, the eleven-year-old William Shakespeare was peering through the railings at Kenilworth Castle and marvelling at the pageant the Earl of Leicester had laid on for the visit of Queen Elizabeth. Sir Walter Raleigh was impressing his friends at court by demonstrating the rituals of smoking a new wonder drug called tobacco. London's first theatre was being opened and Thomas Tallis and William Byrd were celebrating, having just been given the royal monopoly on the production of sheet music. The great houses at Longleat and Burghley, built for aristocratic display rather than defence, were nearing completion. Gaelic-speaking clan chiefs in the Scottish Highlands were taking English lessons and increasingly self-confident parliaments were establishing a national system of parish poor relief. Civil servants rather than soldiers were being elevated to the nobility, civil society was the new big idea and England was rapidly becoming the least militarized country in Europe.[24] All was well with the civilized world. The people who'd been beating each other up on this hillside by the Carter Bar were as foreign as the natives Sir Francis Drake would discover on his world voyage two years later. And the reivers and their families got about as much consideration as those other strange peoples. To civilized society the Border was a primitive world, its residents wild men who'd somehow managed to survive from ancient times. A human Jurassic Park.

The walk out on to Wooplaw Edge, with Arks Edge and Hungry Law up ahead, takes us into a wilderness – one of the last of this endangered species. It's a place one local shepherd

24 John Miller, *Britain, 1600*

described to me simply as 'the loneliness'. There's a path as far as Wooplaw Edge, used by car-weary trippers who stop to stretch their legs at the Carter Bar and ease the kids' travel sickness. And then nothing. But this nothingness served the reivers well. Here they could melt into the folds of the landscape. Here they could catch sight of their pursuers a long way off.

And there was one enemy that rarely caught up with them here. *Pasturella pestis* stalked the land. It raged as close as Carlisle and Berwick and occasionally crept up the Border valleys to communities such as Ednam and Sprouston. But the plague rarely touched the scattered reiving homesteads. Certainly they had their hovels, and hovels harbour disease. Without doubt they had their rats, which inevitably had their fleas, but, more important, the people had little contact with the world beyond the reiving lands and that saved them from the tides of contagion. Up here in the wide views and the clear air you can understand how they got away with it and how they probably joked on the way home across these hills that they'd got themselves a new nickname. Somebody who'd been drinking in Carlisle had overheard them being called 'the Border's own black death', responsible in these parts for more killing than the fearsome disease. Another dubious badge of honour.

Another curse the reivers avoided was the Elizabethan economic disease – inflation. The cost of living, having scarcely risen at all between 1300 and 1500, went up fivefold during Elizabeth's reign.[25] Because the reivers stole what they needed the rise passed them by. Towards the end of the sixteenth century they were living relatively high on the hogget, while their victims in Cumberland and Northumberland struggled below the breadline. In 1578 the Privy Council was forced to

25 C.M.L. Bouch and G.P. Jones, *The Lake Counties 1500–1830*, Manchester University Press, 1961

pay for 1,000 quarters of peas, oats and barley to be shipped from Dorset to prevent starvation among Her Majesty's subjects in Cumberland and Westmorland. And by 1597 the Dean of Durham was reporting that many men had walked all the way from Carlisle to buy bread. If they stuck to the main roads in daylight and kept their fingers crossed they might just have had a chance of getting the loaf home without that, too, being lifted by the reivers.

On the climb out to Hungry Law, there's a grand cairn on the site of what was once Phillips Cross, one of the wayside crosses that marked the tracks through the high country for amateur travellers who'd never learned the reivers' homing instincts. It stands on the line of an old drove road that climbs out of Redesdale and heads north to Jedburgh. Where it crests the shoulder of Catcleugh hill the ground's been cut away to make it passable to wheeled vehicles. Today I'm the only traffic. In fact, sitting up here on the high frontier, leaning against the pile of rocks, it feels as though I'm the only person alive in the vast patterned landscape that rolls away north of Cheviot through the eastern borders.

For light reading on this bit of the journey I'd shoved into my pocket a slim volume about the business of borders that I'd come across by chance in a second-hand bookshop.[26] It turned out to be a collection of anthropological essays, chock full of closely reasoned arguments about ethno-nationalism and post-modernity. I think. Slim it may have been, but light it wasn't.

But under Hungry Law, and with nothing else to read, it turned out to be a treasure trove of facts and fancies about the role of borders in the world. Did you know, for example, that the 185 members of the United Nations (at least there were 185 when the

26 Hastings Donnan and Thomas H. Wilson Berg, *Borders: Frontiers of Identity, Nation and State*, Berg, 1999

book was written in 1999) have 313 land borders between them? Store that away that for future use in Trivial Pursuits.

The lists of border conflicts, dispute and illegality stretch from here to eternity. Armenia and Azerbaijan, Ethiopia and Eritrea, Israel and Lebanon, Greece and Turkey, America and Mexico, Serbia and Bosnia and Croatia. Ethnic mayhem in Nagorno-Karabakh, Zaire and Rwanda, Greece and Albania, Palestine and Israel, Serbia and Albania, the Czech Republic and Romania. Recent border wars in Korea and Vietnam, Laos, Cambodia, India, Pakistan, China, Nigeria and Biafra. Also Chad, Mozambique, Southern Africa and Israel. Border flashpoints in disputes over self-determination and nationhood have involved the Chechens, the Kurds, the Basques, the Sikhs, the Quebecois and the Irish. I've likely forgotten some. But I do remember that, according to the authors, things have been getting worse since 1989.

'Well, at least we managed to sort out most of our differences in the seventeenth century,' I said to no one in particular, there being no one in particular within about five miles of me as I passed the trig point on Hungry Law and headed down over Greyhound Law and the obscurely named Heart's Toe. I know it's probably a bad habit, talking to yourself in the middle of nowhere, but I often do it.

'But the really interesting thing . . . ' Sorry.

The really interesting concept I gleaned from the anthropologists was that borders aren't just places. They're also processes, instruments of state policy and vital elements in the construction and maintenance of national consciousness. And those processes create border mentalities, identities and cultures. They force the people of borders to be different. But I think the Armstrongs and Grahams probably knew that without the help of a passing anthro-apologist.

Borders aren't just lines in the sand (or, in this case, a line in the ankle-threatening white grass tussocks of Ogre Hill that are the present challenge). Borders are also ideas and metaphors and states of mind. As Lord Curzon once said, and the anthropologists duly reported, 'The evolution of frontiers is perhaps an art rather than a science, so plastic and malleable are its forms and manifestations.' It's hard to get a grip of any such idea in a place as empty as this. Art and culture and the border as malleable metaphor all need people. And the people have gone.

At which moment they arrived. Ten or twelve flapping cagoules plodding north along the dreary Pennine Way, which crosses the Border here and then rejoins it for the trip across the high Cheviots. Their hoods were up, giving them the appearance of a squad of grim reapers. Or monks on a forlorn pilgrimage. They were dripping with sweat and misery. Ghosts with leaden legs. They turned out to be salespersons (sadly, that is the word they used) from Manchester, walking the Pennine Way as a management bonding exercise. By the look of them it wasn't working.

'So how come you're not sweating?' asked a pretty lady salesperson with a forced smile, who was carrying as much on her front as she was on her back and who'd obviously been encouraged to join the party to boost the testosterone levels of her dour male companions.

'Because I'm a bone idle walker who sets himself ridiculously low targets.'

'Where are you going?' asked a man who seemed to be on the verge of chronic depression. If not suicide.

'Berwick.'

'And how far's that?'

'About fifty-five or sixty miles.'

'Bugger me. I feel better already,' said he, slouching off in the direction of Kirk Yetholm and a closer, blessed finish. There was no chance of him getting lost and no need for wayside crosses on the Pennine Way. The skid mark through the peat that runs all the way from Edale in Derbyshire achieves motorway proportions in places and for miles it's paved in slabs flown in by helicopter from dismantled Yorkshire mills. One day Pennine Way walkers will be asked to come in carpet slippers and bring a Hoover.

I leaned on my shepherd's crook to reinforce the image of idleness and watched them grumble away to the north. I really should have been looking for the source of the River Coquet, which is half a mile in the opposite direction. Logan Mack did. River sources were compulsory for his party. But I'm afraid I've never really been turned on by damp patches in the grass, which is what incipient rivers tend to be. So instead I breezed off round the contour, joined the infant Coquet anyway and walked beside it to the Roman marching camps at Chew Green.

They're an impressive archaeological muddle – a fort, two fortlets, two camps and a section of Roman road, the marching camps and fortlets overlying each other and obviously all built at different periods. They're also big. The largest of the marching camps encloses more than twenty acres of hill ground and is one of the grandest in Britain. As every reasonably attentive schoolboy knows, when the Roman army was on the move it never halted for even a single night in hostile territory without throwing up a ditched enclosure capable of giving protection to the troops and their baggage train. And this place would certainly have counted as hostile territory in the period when the Romans were trying to keep supply lines open between Hadrian's Wall and their frontier too far – the Antonine Wall, stretching from Forth to Clyde.

Chew Green is almost 1,500 feet above sea level in what would have been the tribal badlands. According to Logan Mack, the biggest of the Chew Green camps was constructed to accommodate an ordinary consular army or two legions with their allies, in all 16,800 foot and 1800 horse. Its general form was square, each side 2017 Roman feet in length (the Roman foot being 11.65 English inches), the whole surrounded by a ditch, the earth dug out being thrown inwards so as to form an embankment, on the top of which was a palisade of the wooden stakes which were carried by each soldier.

You have to wonder what the British made of it all as they stood on their hilltops and watched the Roman squaddies knock up a fully functional camp before tea. It was the imperial equivalent of those scenes in B-movie westerns as the Indians (or Native American peoples, as the Manchester salespersons would doubtless have called them) stood on the skyline and watched the wagon train being driven into a defensive circle for the night. But while you're imagining that, just consider for a moment that our knowledge of the American Plains Indians is complete and comprehensive compared with how little we know about our own ancestors. We have no real grip at all on who the native 'British' people were who were standing on top of the hill and watching the Roman advance.

Worse, we almost know them too well. We're steeped in a belief that they were woad-covered savages who, like as not, grunted as their knuckles trailed the ground. It's an image that suited nineteenth-century Britain very well. It chimed with imperial propaganda. What we were doing to 'civilize' the savages of India and Africa the Romans had done in a far-off time for the wild men of Britain. It's a short step from that to the belief that we smart, modern people are the inheritors of the Roman mantle and that everything before the Romans is best forgotten. You know it makes sense because Roman writers and imperial historians have told us so.

To be fair to the Romans – something I'm not normally accused of – the cult of Romanitas, of the British wrapping themselves in the Roman memory, started early. In the sixth century Celtic cavalry generals would ride into battle wearing remnants of Roman armour, a much-darned red cloak flowing from their shoulders and carrying before them the imperial eagle. These were symbols of status instantly recognized by their own troops and unsettling to their enemies. But in a way Romanitas undermined and distorted the belief of the British in their own traditions. The achievements of the pre-Roman Celtic peoples are ignored, though they had a fully functional hierarchical society well enough established for the Romans to have diplomatic contact with them and even accept them as client kingdoms.

While we're at it, a later example of the same thing is that it suited the English very well to demonize the Scots. They thought of them as thick and uncultured with funny clothes and a funnier language. Not quite Johnny Foreigner but the next worst thing. English chroniclers linked them to images of satanic evil. Their viciousness was legend made fact. As late as 1745 Bonnie Prince Charlie's highlanders were reputed to eat children.

Dismount from hobbyhorse outside the fort at Chew Green.

The fort was designed for more permanent occupation than the larger marching camp and it's at places like this that the real story of Romano-British relations would have been acted out. The natives can't have been so revolting because the Romans went to great lengths to negotiate with them and even employ them. More important still, the Romans needed them as suppliers of food and labour. By the time the fort was up and running Roman quartermasters would be organizing provision deals with the locals and offering a bit of employment as fetchers and carriers. The Romans had a sneaking respect for the British ability to rob them blind when they were haggling over the price of grain or cattle.

The neighbourhood tribal boss would be invited to the odd cocktail party in the Roman fort. When the invitation came his wife would wonder what she was going to wear. When she got home after the party she would want to have her hair done in the same style as the Roman commander's wife. Before you knew it there would be scarcely a spit of difference between the people inside the fort and the people outside. And that's in large part how the Roman conquest of Britain worked. More fashion than fighting. It was more likely to happen like that in the big permanent garrisons along the Roman wall. There the British were taken on as auxiliary troops. Sons followed fathers into the job. After twenty-five years' service they got a sort of Roman citizenship. But even here, at a remote outpost like Chew Green, it's inconceivable that, as time went on, there weren't well-developed economic and even social contacts.

The bonding salespersons caught up with me again at Chew Green, having taken the official but rather silly Pennine Way detour to Coquet Head. I made sure I was still leaning idly on the crook as they climbed up through the earthworks. They were looking two miles more miserable. They stopped to have lunch and I joined them. My sandwiches were a disgrace compared with theirs. Mine were crumpled corned beef and pickle, which I offered round but found no takers. Theirs looked like the remains of a Fortnum and Mason hamper and were delicious. Try as I might, I couldn't think of anywhere within thirty miles of Chew Green where you could get rocket and roasted vegetable sandwiches and containers of salad Niçoise as a carry-out. Presumably they'd lugged them all the way from Manchester.

It started to drizzle again, so we compared weather horror stories. They'd been wet through for most of their trip. The lady did what was obviously her morale-boosting party piece about how she'd had to wring out her bra at one overnight stop. It was a cheering image but it didn't stop one particularly surly member of the squad suggesting that weathermen should be shot. He obviously wasn't aware that meteorologists are a fearsome breed. Joseph Stalin trained as a weatherman.

After they'd packed up their delicatessen and gone, I mooched about for a while in the long grass around the camps looking for traces of Dere Street. It was cut through here in the first century AD on the orders of the first Roman Governor of Britain, Julius Agricola. It ran from York to Perthshire. Logan Mack repeated a mistake made by eighteenth-century scholars and identified the road as Watling Street, which was actually the Roman route from London to Wales with an extension from London to Dover. Quite why the names got muddled up is a bit of a puzzle. The name Dere Street is probably Anglo-Saxon, meaning the forest way. If the Romans gave it a name, it was likely to have been the Via Domitiana, after Titus Flavius Domitianus, the emperor of the day. But for simplicity's sake let's just call it Dere Street.

It's still possible to trace the line of the road across the hill above Chew Green, and among the remains of the marching camps you can find the outline of a fortlet that was kept in service for much longer than the rest of the Roman works as a guard post and road-repair depot. What I couldn't find was any sign of the medieval village of Kemylpethe, which grew up in the ruins of Chew Green.

For thirty years I've been drawn to the period that's sloppily known as the Dark Ages. The interest started on hungover, dressing-gowned Saturday mornings in the sun-drenched bay window of a first-floor flat in Mayfair Mansions, Manchester. The juice from Manx kippers and Oxford marmalade dripped on to Ordnance Survey maps laid out across the breakfast table as my flatmate of the time, the historian Michael Wood, set out passionately held theories about the (to him obvious) continuity of settlement and civil society after the departure of the Romans. His boundless enthusiasms were brighter than the morning as girlfriends of the time whispered round the flat, tidying up after the party of the night before. Maybe that's why I've always thought of the Dark Ages as a sensual time. Mike's thesis was that the shift from Roman rule was an almost seamless transfer of power. He was fascinated by southern settlements like St Albans. My imagination was flying across the Borders.

Imagine a garrison on the frontier towards the end of the Roman occupation. Regular troops were being steadily withdrawn to fight imperial adventures in Gaul. British auxiliaries were left to hold the fort. Their families were living in the *vicus*, the civil settlement outside the gates. After some years of being told by what remained of Roman central command that the cheque was in the post the soldiers had had enough. They decided they'd go it alone. They'd use the skills they'd been taught by the Romans to set up their own frontier protection force. The protection money they managed to extract from their neighbours would make up for the lack of wages. Within a matter of decades they'd become Border reivers, even though they wouldn't be called that for another fifteen hundred years. In the intervening period they practised their techniques as the shock troops of Celtic Britain, leading the charge in the doomed campaigns to hold back the advancing Anglo-Saxons. One of their home-grown commanders was a chap who would eventually be called Arthur, who died at the battle of Camlann. That was almost certainly fought at the crooked glen where the River Irthing runs by the site of the Roman fort at Birdoswald. And don't take a blind bit of notice of what the people of Wales and south-west England will tell you to the contrary.

If the lads of Liddesdale and Tynedale had been interested in such frills, this real Arthur could easily have been adopted as the patron saint of the reivers.

At Birdoswald on the Roman Wall archaeologists have discovered what's been described as a Dark Ages wooden hall built in the ruins of the fort. Clear evidence that things were brighter than we've imagined. Life went on in some style. The useful bits of Roman experience were treasured and handed on from father to son – cavalry tactics, military discipline, understanding the enemy. The froth of imperial life was largely abandoned – reading and writing, building in stone in a cold, wet climate, bathing and importing that horrible fish paste from the Mediterranean.

Whether or not a similar slow dissolve from Rome to Britain happened here at Kemylpethe I don't know, but there's certainly evidence of continuing use of the site as late as the sixteenth century. A cluster of redundant Roman buildings beside a well-used road in the middle of sheep-grazing territory would have attracted occupants. I just don't buy the Dark Ages argument that this was too dangerous a place to live after the withdrawal of Rome's civilizing presence. If trouble was a barrier to occupation nobody would have lived in Liddesdale and Tynedale and Redesdale in the sixteenth century.

The 1550 Border Survey refers to houses built 'in times past called Kemylpethe Walls'.[27] By the sixteenth century, it had given its name – by then Gamelspath – to a stretch of the Dere Street highway. The English and Scots Wardens recognized it as a traditional trysting place and set it as the officially recognized rendezvous for offenders from Coquetdale and Redesdale who faced trial by single combat. An excavation in 1883 found the

27 My thanks to Piers Dixon, who gave me access to his unpublished Ph.D. thesis 'The Deserted Mediaeval Villages of North Northumberland'

remains of a building, identified as a chapel, within one of the fortlets and a local shepherd discovered a cross head on the hillside near by. Kelso Abbey held the grazing rights here from 1227, so it's conceivable that they established a chapel of ease in this little pastoral community to keep God's thumbprint on the locals. They'd have had their work cut out.

Mammon was certainly hard at it here. His business was done in a wayside tavern at Kemylpethe. It would have been quite a place, full of Scots pedlars selling bridles and linen, spears and stirrups and doing a bit of spying on the side. There would have been a steady flow of itinerant Scots workers – shepherds and colliers looking for jobs in the English Marches. It was illegal for English landowners to employ them, but they did because they could get them cheap. There would have been smugglers and coiners. (Forging Scots currency was such a nice little earner that the Grahams in the English West March employed their own resident coiner.)

It would have been a rumbustious, rancid hole of a place, the customers jabbering in the 'northern tongue', which was part English and part Scots. The distinct dialects we know came much later. Most of the customers wouldn't have washed for some months; in fact the majority of them would have been sewn into their underwear. But nobody would have noticed the constant scratching because they were all doing it. In the same way the heaps of dung and ash at the back door would have been unremarkable because every house had them. Poverty and lawlessness were great levellers.

Who the locals of Kemylpethe were we'll never know, but I bet their DNA survived in the Robsons of Coquet and Tyne and the Halls and Hedleys of Redesdale. There was maybe even a bit of it in the odd travelling Armstrong and Elliot from Liddesdale. The Border bond that we've identified along this frontier could well be in the genes.

CHAPTER TEN

View of Valley by Hen Hole

On the map it's marked as a danger area. The danger no longer comes from reivers and bandits. Today it's from artillery. The line of the Roman Dere Street to the south cuts across the army's Redesdale training range. The militarized zone that was the medieval Border still exists. An earlier traveller, the historian and painter Jessie Mothersole, fought her way the length of Dere Street in the 1920s.[28] She was a spirited lady. When she crossed the ranges she found herself in the middle of a full-scale live firing exercise.

As we walked we could hear the shells whizzing over our heads and then the dull explosion in the distance. We could see rows of dummy men set up to be fired at, and the turf-covered dug-outs of the officers who were watching the effects of the shells. [Sadly she doesn't report the look on the officers' faces as a lady with handbag and brolly walked through their war game.] Farther on we passed a dummy man lying in the grass among the shell holes. We were told that the occupiers of the farms are under orders to take shelter when firing is going on, but that they get so used to it that they do not take the trouble.

I'm told that these days the army takes a dim view of any such bravado during exercises, even if you are a little old lady, so if the red flags are flying keep out.

They weren't. So I didn't. I climbed out along the line of the Roman road to the pass between Harden Edge and Thirl Moor. At 1,674 feet this is where Dere Street reaches the highest point on its hundred and thirty or so miles from York. In front

28 Jessie Mothersole, *Agricola's Road into Scotland*, The Bodley Head, 1927

of me Foulplay Head, but what particular bit of foul play it commemorates is long forgotten. And behind and below me the earthworks of the Chew Green camps, which from this height make rather more sense. Another mile brought me to the Outer Golden Pot. It's a stone socket beside the roadway, probably at one time a base for another wayside cross which also served as a parish boundary marker. It's said that its name comes from legends of a buried treasure. And it's guarded the moor for at least eight hundred years. The first reference to it, when it's described as one of the 'Golding-pottes' that marked the way from Redesdale to Chew Green, is in that early thirteenth-century deed held by Kelso Abbey, which gave the monks a gift of every tenth foal born to the wild mares that roamed the nearby Forest of Cottenshope. The horses have gone, but the ground where they once galloped through the centuries billows away to the east like a thrown sheet of blue green silk, eventually settling across the shoulders of Cheviot.

Back at Chew Green, I was chuntering to myself about how inconsiderate it had been to shut the Kemylpethe pub as I rejoined the Border, which was in dispute in these parts as late as 1840. A map of Roxburghshire produced that year leaves the line past Chew Green blank. Just south of the camp there's a tract of ground called the Plea Shank, which name suggests it had been the subject of disagreement, if not litigation. For centuries it had been a disputed buffer zone between the English Makendon estate, owned in the nineteenth century by Ralph Carr Ellison, and the Scottish property of the Duke of Roxburgh. When the Ordnance Survey made its first map of this wild area it put it into Scotland. Sir Ralph wasn't having it. He trawled the records and found evidence of English occupation in the past. The Ordnance Survey recalled its maps and issued new ones showing a disputed boundary. I've no idea when the dispute was finally settled, but by the time

Logan Mack came through here about sixty years later the Plea Shank was firmly in England.

From Chew Green the Border runs north-west to the watershed and then takes a right-angled turn to the north-east to follow it to Brownhart Law. In its day the Roman signal station on Brownhart Law was part of a state-of-the-art communications network, using beacons and perhaps even semaphore to keep forts on the Roman wall in touch with the goings-on at their remote northern outposts at Rubers Law and Trimontium. The system was set up to warn of emergencies, but, like e-mails today, you can bet the bulk of the messages that flapped or flared across the hills were concerned with administrative dross or silly jokes. The butt of those would be about the 'Britunculi' – the thick little Brits. The Romans may have had high-level diplomatic contact with the British but that was no reason not to laugh at us foreigners. Such jokes were just a natural forerunner of stories about the Irish, the Poles and anyone who comes from Runcorn.

Beyond Brownhart Law we're heading into a world of gods and mysteries. By Greystone Brae and Gaisty Law, with lingering views down into the valley of the Hindhope Burn, we're following the line of Dere Street out to Black Halls Hill. The boss god here was Woden, the god of war and imagination, and the north-western horizon is dominated by Woden Law. Surprisingly, Logan Mack scarcely mentions it in *The Border Line*, but it's worth the detour.

For many years the mystery of Woden Law was why the Romans had bothered to lay siege to so insignificant a native camp. The Iron Age fort at the summit covers scarcely more than an acre, ringed by defensive rubble walls. It was the sort of place that would normally have been bought off by Roman negotiation. If its inhabitants had been bold enough or daft enough to resist, a modest legionary force could have overrun it on a Wodensday afternoon. But on the slopes approaching the camp there are spectacular Roman siegeworks, built seventy feet or so away from the fort's defensive ramparts – just beyond the killing range of hand-thrown missiles.[29] There are assault platforms and emplacements for siege engines and tracks by which these *ballistae* were hauled into position. All laid out in clearly defined sectors across the hill slopes. On a smaller scale they replicate the techniques discovered at the greatest Roman siege site in the world at Masada on the edge of the Judaean desert in Israel. In AD 73 the Roman tenth legion besieged Masada's rock fortress, where more than a thousand Jewish zealots had taken refuge after the fall of Jerusalem. The Roman army had developed siege tactics that didn't rely on simply starving the garrison into submission. It was siege and attack. Eventually, threatened with being overrun, the defenders of Masada committed suicide rather than fall under the power of Rome. The state of Israel disappeared for almost nineteen hundred years. But why would the Roman legions in obscure north Britain find it necessary to employ the same tactics? What was so special about Woden Law?

Then the *denarii* dropped. The siegeworks at Woden Law weren't real. It was a training ground. What the British Army is doing today four or five miles away in Redesdale the Romans were doing here eighteen hundred years ago. They'd picked one of the bleakest spots in the Borders to toughen up their troops. Close to the main trunk road of northern Britain and with camps near by at Pennymuir where the squaddies could be billeted, it was the perfect place. No doubt the poor bloody infantry would have held a rather different view and the parentage of their officers would probably have been a

29 Sir Ian Richmond and Professor J.K.S. St Joseph, *Society of Antiquaries of Scotland 112*, 1982

matter of vigorous debate as they trudged back to Pennymuir in a snowstorm after a hard day's besieging.

Now, far be it from me to be nanny statist, but this is as good a moment as any to point out that the next long stretch of the Border isn't for the faint-hearted. If you even have to consider whether or not you'll make it, you probably won't. We're talking twenty and more miles of high-level walking. It's a day's work in anybody's book. Certainly in this one. There are tracks off the hill along the way, but most of them involve ten miles to anywhere. So I'd arranged to be picked up from the back roads below Woden Law and taken for a night's rest and recuperation before heading for the high Cheviots.

The theory was fine. As, indeed, was the company. After dinner I fell in with an accountant from Leeds and a lady rep from Pontefract who was selling industrial detergents. However unpromising that may sound, they turned out to be surprisingly good fun and we three lonely foreigners, who had in common that we were being studiously ignored by the locals, chatted about this and that. George, the accountant, was advising some company in the Borders about tax planning but was much more interested in talking about his heroine Cartamandua. She was Queen of the Brigantes, the tribe that controlled the territory from north of the Tweed Valley to where Doncaster and Sheffield stand now. She's often called the northern Boadicea. George assured me that in accountancy circles they talk of little else.

Cartamandua is best known for her betrayal of the Celtic freedom fighter Caratacus to the Roman invaders. George was determined to put a rather different spin on the story. According to him, Cartamandua was just fulfilling the terms of a diplomatic treaty she'd negotiated with Rome. Whatever the excuses, the outcome was same. Caratacus was hauled off to Italy to be put on public display as the savage who had bravely stood in the way of the imperial advance. According to the Roman historian Tacitus, the Emperor was so impressed by the British leader that he gave him his freedom. At that meeting Caratacus is reported as saying, 'If you Romans choose to conquer the world, does it follow that the world should accept slavery?'

We stayed on safer ground. Back home in Brigantia, Cartamandua had spotted a business opportunity. Why fight the Romans when you can sell to them? At Stanwick in Yorkshire she built the equivalent of a Freeport, an 800-acre trading post where the Brigantians dealt in lead and cattle and grain. As Cartamandua had several tens of thousands of armed supporters, we agreed that very few people left without paying. Isobel the detergent, who until that moment had never heard of Cartamandua, immediately adopted her as a mascot. She reckoned that arriving with a squad of armed-to-the-teeth Brigantians would help her sales figures no end. As she headed for bed she tapped her hip pocket as in the supermarket adverts, smiled broadly and shouted, 'Brigantes price.' An ominous silence descended and George and I crept out of the bar.

Unfortunately for me, my drinking companions only had to walk as far as the car the next morning. I was going a bit further. As a result of the minor excesses of the night before and a lack of sleep my second acquaintance with Woden Law was less pleasant than the first.

Instead of doing the sensible thing and following Dere Street round the contour to Black Halls Hill, I decided, in a fuddled sort of way, to take the direct route back to the Border. An hour later I was still mired in the bogs of Scraesburgh Hope. I was wet to the knees by the time I got to Raeshaw Fell. And it wasn't laughter. For a brief moment I thought how pleasant it must be to gossip over the photocopier while someone rushed to make the morning coffee. Then I remembered the constantly ringing telephones and the storm of meaningless e-mails, the Neanderthal line manager and the other delights of office life. And suddenly I was in demi-paradise on Raeshaw Fell.

It's another of those spots where Border disputes and land use patterns of hundreds of years ago are still writ large on the map. A great chunk of what, logically, would seem to be a bit of Scotland – a block of ground a mile square – has been bolted on to England. Logan Mack speculates that what we're seeing is the demarcation of an ancient royal deer park. He's backed up by the modern maps where there are echoes of the chase – Dormount Hope (a corruption of Deermount) and Deer Doups and Deer Cleuch.

At one stage, perhaps as early as the thirteenth century, the Border ran further south across what Logan Mack called not Raeshaw but Rushy Fell. That earlier boundary was marked by a broad ditch cut out of the peat. How far it went we don't really know, but the best surviving bit is here. It's a place and a moment when you can't help stopping in your tracks and imagining the years of spadework serfdom in all weathers that were involved in its making. Particularly when you see it beside the puny wire fence that diffidently marks the Border today. The ditch diggers would likely have taken a rather different view. They would have marvelled at the simple, technological advance that was barbed wire.

But it would be another six hundred years before, in 1873, Lucinda Glidden of Dekalb, Illinois, one day persuaded her husband to think of something to keep the cows out of her garden. Using a converted coffee grinder to bend wire spikes he came up with an invention that the Plains Indians and religious groups condemned as 'the devil's rope' but which dramatically changed frontiers around the world. At last there was a cheap and effective way of turning space into place.

We're walking the wire to Lamb Hill and Beefstand Hill and Mozie Law. For most of the next twenty miles or so we'll be on the Pennine Way with its paving and duckboards and slithering, eroded peat. Ahead there's the rollercoaster of summits from Windy Gyle to The Schil. And in every other direction there are wide-angled views over the Borderlands. Bleak moorland running into England. Scotland gentler and more fertile with cloud patterns drifting across rounded hills from Peeblesshire to the valley of the Tweed. The whole slow-motion scene wrapped in the silence of the dead.

But judging by the evidence underfoot it's not always as quiet as this. Everywhere there are scramble bike tracks where riders have bounced and skidded through the peat to demonstrate how well they're coping with their recent lobotomy.

Beyond a kink in the Border at Plea Knowe the frontier jumps to the north for half a mile along the line of a broad and well-preserved drove road called simply the Street. It's another of those threads of continuity in the warp and weft of the landscape tapestry. In its earliest form it would have been a trod by way of which the first settlers in the Bowmont Valley walked their flocks out on to the hill pastures about three and a half thousand years ago. Fifteen hundred years later Roman engineers would have marked it on their maps as a potential route of march over the Cheviots. In the sixth century British warlords would know it as a way south for cavalry detachments setting out to oppose the advancing Anglo-Saxons. A thousand years after the Arthurian defeat that drove the Celtic tribes south and west into the fastnesses of Wales, the Scottish reivers brought cattle stolen from Coquetdale this way, and in the eighteenth and nineteenth centuries their descendants, the drovers, adopted it when lowland enclosure and the development of turnpike toll roads forced them out on to the hills. On Roy's map dating from 1755 this route across the Cheviots was marked as Clattering Path, a boisterous thoroughfare alive with the ringing of cattle shoes and the blasphemies of free-spirited drovers. Today the clattering's stopped. The Street is having another of its routine quiet spells at present, but who knows what the future holds for such an enduring highway?

It's a steady flog to the summit of Windy Gyle along a track marked by grassy cairns and places with names and symbols on the map that offer up hints and whispers of past horrors and long-forgotten superstitions. There's the steep col at Foul Step. But who lost their footing and came to grief there? There's the sharp watershed ridge above Rowhope Burn with the remains of a mysterious earthwork running not along the line but at right angles to the Border. Beyond that there's an acute turn of the frontier to the north again at a place called Split the Deil. Is that an echo, far from home, of the Galloway folktale of Jupiter sending a bolt of lightning that split a chunk of granite and killed the Devil? Is it a remnant of the folk memory of the people who dug the Fosse of the Galwegians far to the west on Christianbury Crag? Or could it just be a tautological muddle of language derived from a Gaelic or more distant root where the word deil could mean to split or sever?[30] Of course the name could be nothing more than a touch of modern whimsy. Certainly Logan Mack makes no mention of Split the Deil at all in *The Border Line*. The name has appeared or returned in the past eighty years.

It was blowing a hooley by the time I got to the cairned summit of Windy Gyle, which at least has a footnote of traceable history associated with it. It was famous for five

---

30 Alexander MacBain, *An Etymological Dictionary of the Gaelic Language*, Gairm Publications, 1982. Similar words to *deil*, meaning an axle or a rod, apparently turn up in old Irish and Cornish and Breton.

minutes at a day of truce on 27 July 1585. That's about the time it took to despatch Lord Francis Russell. Now, murder was a commonplace in the blood-soaked Borderlands of the 1580s. They were seriously troubled times. This was the decade that saw the execution of Mary, Queen of Scots and the threat from the Armada. Always with an eye to the main chance, the Border families, English and Scots, made merry whenever there was a climate of international uncertainty. Lawlessness moved up a gear. But Russell's murder was something else and it caused a serious diplomatic incident. It could easily have sparked an Anglo-Scottish war had it not been for the fact that King James had the English throne in his sights.

Russell was the son-in-law of the English Middle March Warden, Sir John Forster. On that particular day of truce at Windy Gyle (or, more likely, at Hexpethgate Head a couple of miles to the east, which was the regular Middle March meeting point) Forster was wading through the usual complaints and grievances with his Scottish counterpart, the equally untrustworthy Sir Thomas Kerr of Ferniehurst, 'a man of strong anti-English prejudice'. The local rascalry were being dealt with, pledges entered, promises made, fingers crossed. Then suddenly there was a shot and Russell was dead.

The Scots version of events was that it all started when an English lad stole a pair of Scottish spurs. Incensed by so heinous a crime, fah de lah, the Scots charged and Russell was caught in the crossfire.

There were two English versions. At first Forster said it was Russell's fault for meddling at the truce day. But having slept on it he realized the story would play much better with his bosses in London if he could implicate Ferniehurst. He constructed a complex tale of espionage and double-dealing that was partly based on fact. Ferniehurst did indeed have a grudge against Russell, who had intercepted some of his secret correspondence and passed it on to London. But by the time Forster had finished he'd involved not just the Scottish Warden but also King James's favourite of the time, James Stewart, Earl of Arran, the Lord Warden General of all the Scottish Marches. After protests from Queen Elizabeth's Secretary of State and spymaster, Sir Francis Walsingham, King James reluctantly gave way and banished the pair of them. Forster no doubt rejoiced in his good day's work. Maximum embarrassment had been caused to 'The King of Fife', as James was widely known in the Borders, and Forster's son-in-law (whom he didn't much like anyway) at least got a cairn named after him.

In fact there are two giant cairns on Windy Gyle and over the years different mapmakers have called one or other of them Russell's Cairn. Some historians have even suggested that the cairn below the summit marks the very spot where Russell fell. Complete baloney, of course, given that both the cairns are sites of Bronze Age burial rather than sixteenth-century murder.

And sitting here in a whistling wind surrounded by the field of stones I've got to say it's not the stiffening corpse of Russell but clouded images of that ancient moment of mourning that creep into the imagination. A man, his body folded into a foetal position and wrapped in a shroud, is carried by his sons to the open cist on the mountaintop. Other men, cousins and nephews, carry the grave goods that will go with him to the far world. A decorated earthenware cup filled with food for the crossing. Precious metal and stone objects blessed to protect him from the daemons he'll encounter on his final journey from the hills. And all accompanied by the wailing wake of mother and sisters and the Cheviot winds. And, when the body's in place on its bed of bog myrtle, its head to the north, they drag the grave cover into place and start to lay the stones.

For days they build the cairn that gradually separates them from the man who was their leader and their inspiration. And for the rest of their lives they'll look up from the valley and see his memory etched against the sky.

Of course that's a flight of fancy, too, but at least mine isn't three thousand years adrift.

It's a gentle descent with a following wind along a cairned path to the Border Gate – the place that was known as Hexpethgate in Russell's time. For hundreds if not thousands of years this has been one of the main crossing points of the Cheviots. This cross-border roadway linking Kelso with Morpeth is shown as Clennel Street on the modern fingerpost and described as Roman in most guides, but it's had any number of other names and as many suggested origins. In droving days it was Emspeth or Ermspeth – the path of the eagle. It was also known as the Salter's Path, linking South Shields with the Borders at a time when Shields reputedly produced the finest salt in Britain using cheap supplies of coal to evaporate sea water. In the 1630s a traveller along the Salter's road reported that there were 250 houses in Shields engaged in the salt trade. Each house had 'one fair great pan' which made a handsome profit of £2 10s. a week.[31]

But the better profits were to be had from smuggling salt across the Border into Scotland. It was Mary, Queen of Scots who first introduced a salt tax. Queen Elizabeth soon caught on to the idea but rates of duty varied between the two countries and they were usually higher in Scotland. After dark, at lonely Border crossings like Clennel Street, smugglers would take salt north and bring whisky back. It happened all the way along this leaky frontier. At Kirk Yetholm, up ahead,

31 Sir William Brereton, 'Notes of a Journey Through Northumberland and Durham in the Year 1635', private letter books

where we'll drop in from the Cheviot watershed, it was reckoned that one person in five was involved in the smuggling trade. In the west, even after the salt tax was abolished in the 1820s, Longtown and Newcastleton were smugglers' havens and you can bet your life it was descendants of the reiving Armstrongs and Elliots and Grahams who were masterminding it. In 1825 the *Carlisle Journal* reported that

> On the 25th inst. Messrs Gilchrist, Coulson and Marshall, officers of the Excise at Springfield and Annan, seized near Newcastleton a hearse and two horses, the vehicle, instead of a dead body, having within a living spirit, in the shape of thirty gallons of prime Scotch whiskey, which the cunning driver was merrily trotting towards England.

A paved track, replaced through some of the wetter bits by duck boarding, leads from beyond the Border Gate to the summit of Cheviot. In Logan Mack's day the Border here was marked by little heaps of stones along the fence line. The modern fixtures and fittings amount almost to a loss of innocence.

Cheviot is an English mountain. The Border veers off to the left across its shoulder, once again leaving several square miles of Scotland lying south of England. Cheviot is also a galumphing and boring summit, scarcely worth the three-mile detour to visit it unless you're a mountain trainspotter. Logan Mack would have disagreed. He reckoned that from a distance and with a sprinkling of snow it's the spit of the Jungfrau as seen from Interlaken. Never having seen the Jungfrau from Interlaken or anywhere else, I'll have to take his word for it. But even he had to admit that standing in the middle of the Cheviot summit plateau was a bit like being a fly in the centre of a table. Certainly, if you get the weather, there can be grand, distant views from points on the edge of the plateau, but no better than from other summits along the Border.

One famous visitor to Cheviot has left us an account of an ascent which will fill in the views you're going to miss. Daniel Defoe (Logan Mack insists on his real name – Daniel Foe) went to the top on horseback.

The day happened to be very clear, and to our great satisfaction very calm, otherwise the height we were upon would not have been without its dangers. We saw plainly here the smoke of the salt pans at Shields, at the mouth of the Tyne, seven miles below Newcastle; and which is about forty miles. The sea, that is the German Ocean, was as if but just at the foot of the hill, and our guide pointed to show us the Irish Sea. But if he could see it, knowing it in particular and where exactly to look for it, it was so distant, that I could not say I was assured I saw it.

Which is hardly surprising. Mr Foe's account impressed Logan Mack mightily but even he had to point out that from where the great man stood to Port Patrick is 128 miles. Catching sight of it would have needed not so much twenty-twenty vision as computer graphics.

While we're in Daniel Defoe's company it's perhaps worth mentioning that he took an interest in the Border that went beyond mere sightseeing. He was one of the influential writers who, in the early eighteenth century, helped bring about the union of the English and Scottish Parliaments and the downgrading of the frontier. His passionately argued pamphlets outlining the economic case for union helped sway apathetic Scots opinion.

Much better than Cheviot's dreary, rounded top are two of the grandest features of the whole Cheviot range lying just below it. Off to the right of the path is the Hanging Stone.

Until the sixteenth century the Border ran through it and from as early as the twelfth century it was the recognized dividing point between the Middle and East Marches. When the Border was moved to the watershed, the Hanging Stone was left stranded in England. Nowadays a mound on the watershed 250 yards to the north of it marks the point where the Border line reaches its greatest elevation – 2,439 feet.

It's said in some descriptions of the Border that the Hanging Stone got its name because a pedlar or smuggler was accidentally hanged from one of its rocks when the strap of his pack slipped round his neck. Another fancy of the Border folklorists that stuck, I fear. It's actually named the way it looks. Tall rocks riven and hanging at crazy angles after some volcanic upheaval or glacial scouring.

I have bad memories of the Hanging Stone. On an earlier visit I'd flogged up from the valley with a camera crew specifically to film it. The weather was perfect. The company was good.

The stone was casting its shadows across the hill and had a skyscape behind it that couldn't have been more perfect if Claude himself had painted it. At which point the camera broke down. Thirty-six thousand pounds worth of camera that wouldn't take even a happy snap.

'Gosh what a shame,' said I.

Jan the cameraman tried to look on the bright side but it was F2.8 rather than F16. He said that at least he could get a mobile phone signal up here, so he could order a new camera for tomorrow.

'Five miles down and five miles back up again,' said I. 'Gosh, what a shame.'

I never did get back to the Hanging Stone. Until now. The skyscape isn't as good and the shadows aren't as clear cut, but at least I'll take away more in my mind's eye than Jan did in his Ikegami. Which is presumably Japanese for chocolate fireguard.

Doubling back on itself, the Border line heads straight to the sprawling stone-field of Auchope Cairn. It's said you can see Lochnagar 105 miles away from here, which sounds almost as dodgy a proposition as Mr Foe's views of Port Patrick. In *The Border Line* Auchope Cairn is notable because of a photograph of the author and his photographer. Logan Mack is dressed in dark suit and tie with polished shoes and wearing a black homburg. His cameraman looks the double of Robert Louis Stevenson when he'd gone native. Gleaming high boots and colonial jacket topped off with a jaunty wide-brimmed hat to emphasize his creative credentials. But how on earth did they get to Auchope Cairn looking like that? I was mud and crumple by the time I stumbled up the final slope to lean on the same stone pillar. Logan Mack 1, Robson 0.

After Auchope Cairn the Border takes off down the side of the great ravine of the Cheviots. The hanging valley of Hen Hole. Its other name is Hell's Hole and that suits it better. It's a place where the sun never shines, a chasm of rocks that holds patches of snow into high summer in the shadows by the waterfalls of the College Burn. It was a hiding place of choice for outlaws and reivers and smugglers. In its busy days the innocent traveller who stumbled across Hell's Hole was unlikely to stumble much further and, if he did, he wouldn't be taking his wallet and his watch with him. The raven and the fox have it to themselves now.

There's a knee-jarring 800-feet descent of its southern flank and, just to make sure the cartilages are back in place, a grunt out to the mountain refuge hut that looks across the valley into the mouth of hell. It's a sweet place to sit in the afternoon sunshine. There's the occasional Pennine Way trudger to nod to, but the sensible souls sharing the view with you are

Cheviot sheep on the lookout for a sandwich. When one isn't forthcoming they throw sideways looks of utter disdain. The hut is basic. A wooden board to sleep on and wooden ledges with a visitor's book full of the usual platitudes. 'Great walk or least it will be when it stops' and 'Wet again' and 'Lost George today but he's found us'. There's even a bit of what passes for Pennine Way poetry:

Roses are red, violets are blue,
My anorak's leaking and so's my shoe.

There are scraps left by previous passers-by. An end of candle and a tea bag. An almost empty tin of deodorant, presumably left by someone who'd given up the struggle to be sweet-smelling in the Cheviots, and a packet of digestive biscuits. And two walnuts and a plastic bottle of water. I'm tempted to whip up a fragrant walnut crumble for the next benighted visitor but a sideways glance from a grazing Cheviot puts a stop to that. If you doubt that a sheep can say with some eloquence 'stupid boy' you've never met the stately Cheviot ewe of Hell's Hole.

I head for the Schil and Black Hag and White Law. You'll have gathered I've got a sniff of the end of the day. The delights of Kirk Yetholm beckon. Head down, cover the ground. In truth one bit of this ground looks very much like another. Even the wayward Border is behaving itself for once, dutifully sticking to the watershed and marked by fence and wall until we reach Whitelaw Nick, where it suddenly runs arrow straight and due north for about a mile and a half, presumably the result of another arbitrated land ownership dispute.

These lonely miles on the tail end of the Cheviot section of our trip may have less obvious history crowding in on them, but we still have shadowy cartographic companions. Who or what was the madam of Madam Law, the maddie of Maddie's Well and the tuppie of Tuppie's Grave?

Near the place where poor Tuppie left his final mark on the landscape the Pennine Way bolts for the valley and there's another ancient Border marker. Logan Mack dates the Stob Stanes from the thirteenth century. Far be it from me to quibble, but they look much older. Near by there's a hint of the twin turf dykes that the Border surveyors Bowes and Ellerker identified in 1542 as the 'dytche called the marche dyke'. The turf is thrown up from two parallel ditches with a no-man's-land between them. A notional demilitarized zone broad enough for representatives of the two nations to meet and discuss their differences on neutral territory.

And it seems there was never any shortage of matters to discuss. In the notes of their survey Bowes and Ellerker report that this section of the Border was regularly abused by the Scots, who routinely cultivated English land and drove their sheep and cattle to pasture on the English side in defiance of international law. Scots farmers 'in sundry places plowed down the said old marche dyke of intent to deface and put the same out of knowledge and thereby to encroache of the grounde of England'.

The straight frontier line from Whitelaw Nick across Stob Rig is the final (or at least present) resolution of those disputes that bickered on for more than four hundred years.

On the stroll to Kirk Yetholm I caught up with another struggling Pennine Way walker, a history teacher from somewhere near Glasgow, who was doing the walk because of a boozy bet.

'And I'm never going to bloody well drink again. Apart from the ten pints I'm going to have tonight.'

I told him that the old landlord at the Border Hotel in Kirk Yetholm regularly found complete sets of walking gear in his dustbins abandoned by people who, having finished the Pennine Way, had resolved never to walk again except from the bar stool to the gents. He said he was seriously tempted to do the same if he could find a shop in the village where he could buy a pair of slippers and a pipe. I asked how he was planning to get home to Glasgow.

'My wife's driving down to collect me to check if I've survived my mid-life crisis. She says she's had a very relaxing fortnight reading the life insurance policies.'

The conversation wandered on to Border history, as it would with a captive history teacher trying to take his mind off his blisters. He had a theory that the Union of the Crowns and the subsequent Act of Union were a bit like the reunification of Germany, with Scotland cast in the role of the backward German Democratic Republic.

His argument was that, for centuries, the English thought the Scots were barbaric and ignorant, and a bit of Divine Right jiggery-pokery with James I didn't put a stop to that. Reality kicked in. English industries and merchants were streets ahead of the Scots, so when the new United Kingdom became a free market they cleaned up. The English Parliament had forced through the Act of Union by threatening to ban Scottish imports, which would have brought the Scots economy to its knees. Then there were the new, punitive taxes to pay for the War of the Spanish Succession in the opening years of the eighteenth century – a war to stop Louis XIV's ambition to unite France and Spain, which would have upset the delicate balance of power in Europe. The taxes fell most heavily on the poorer Scots. Unemployment and economic stagnation in Scotland led to riots in Glasgow and Edinburgh. The cream of Scottish talent went to England and ended up running the British Empire.

'And we're not talking the Dark Ages here. Scotland's still looked on as a dependency of England with higher unemployment and knackered industry and a begging-bowl economy . . .'

'Hang on,' says I, never having been one to accept the ideas of teachers without quibble. 'I thought Scotland had a whale of a time after the Union, exporting black cattle for the navy. And tobacco – Glasgow was called tobaccolopolis for a bit – and linen and coal. They never had it so good.'

'Not until the 1760s at the very earliest and even then it didn't last. The point I'm making' – he reinforced it by kicking at an entirely innocent clump of sieves – 'is that the Border became a sort of Berlin Wall that's kept the Scots as the poor relations.'

'Give over,' says I, stung by the rising Anglophobia. 'Since the Union we haven't been able to move for bloody Scots running things. Everybody from Jardine Matheson to Tony Blair. The Scottish Raj, Jeremy Paxman called it.'

'Aye, well maybe you're right about the merchant bankers and New Labour. Bugger all difference between them.'

The cold warrior got into his stride even though he was limping. He said the Border, like the Berlin Wall, was as much a state of mind as a physical frontier. The England–Scotland Border was a line on the map which by all logic should have disappeared after the Act of Union. Instead it became a symbol of capitalist oppression and domination that showed the Scots who was boss.

While his tattered remnant of socialist Scotland continued to flutter over the closed shipyards of red Clydeside, I contented myself with images of Archie Fire the Braes and Buggerback and Nebless Clem Crosier picked out by searchlights as they scaled a concrete wall with a sheep under each arm and cut the barbed wire with their teeth while Erich Honecker sang 'A man's a man for a' that'. A stupid thought which got me to the safety of the Border Hotel, where half-baked history sailed away on a sea of best bitter.

At dusk I went for a walk through Kirk Yetholm, which is a tidy little place huddled round its village green. But when Logan Mack visited in the 1920s he said it had the appearance 'if not of a deserted village, at least of one in the process of extinction. Many wholly or partially ruined and roofless cottages are crumbling earthwards without any attempt being made towards reconstruction or repair.'

A century earlier it hadn't been much better.

The church, low, and covered with thatch, beyond which appears the straggled houses built in the old Scottish style, many of them with their gable ends, backs or corners turned to the street; and still further up the Tinkler Row with its low unequal straw covered roofs and chimneys bound with rushes and hay ropes, men and women loitering at their doors or lazily busied amongst their carts and panniers, and ragged children scrambling on the midden-steads (which rise before every cottage) in intimate and equal fellowship with pigs, poultry, dogs and cuddies.[32]

Even the town's most prestigious resident in the 1870s described it as 'Sae mingle-mangle that ane might think it was built on a dark night or sown on a windy day.'

Yet in those days Kirk Yetholm was a royal capital and the resident in question was Esther Faa Blyth, undisputed Queen of the Gypsies. She'd been undisputed ever since she beat her sister in a bare-knuckle fight on the village green in 1861.

It's said the gypsies came to Kirk Yetholm at the end of the seventeenth century. Before that they'd been an outcast tribe in Scotland, travelling the country telling fortunes, selling illicit gin and liberating any property that wasn't fully bolted down. But a gypsy mercenary saved the life of the Laird of Yetholm,

32 Bailey Smith of Kelso, *Blackwood's Magazine*, May 1817

Captain David Bennett, at the siege of Namur in 1695. In gratitude he gifted some cottages in the village which the gypsies could use as winter quarters. Upwards of 250 of them settled here. They even built a tiny gypsy palace for their royal family, The Lords and Earles of Little Egipt, as they were known.

The gypsies fitted in well in the Borders. Any number of them were hanged for theft or murder. Like the reivers before them, they were clannish and self-sufficient and contemptuous of authority. An account of them written in the 1830s could have been describing the riding families of three hundred years earlier.

> I think it deserving of remark, that most of the murders for which gipsies have been condemned seem to have been committed upon persons of their own tribe, in the heat and violence of passion, the consequence of some old family feud, or upon strangers of other clans for invading what they regard as their territory. Their character for truth and honesty is certainly not high. Their pilfering and plundering habits, practised chiefly when from home, are pretty generally known . . . There is a species of honour among them that, if trusted, they will not deceive . . . A deep spirit of revenge is the darkest trait in their character.[33]

Like the reivers, the gypsies knew how to read the landscape and they were consummate horsemen. As happened to the reivers before them, progress and politics began to hem them in. Many of the gypsy families – Faa and Young and Blyth – emigrated to frontier America, where their skill with horses was in demand. As tractors became the agricultural horsepower of choice in the more prosperous northern states they drifted to the poorer south. Which is why a little boy

33 New Statistical Account for Roxburgh 1834

called William Jefferson Blyth was born in Arkansas. His father had died. His mother remarried someone called Clinton, whose adopted son became Governor in the State House in Little Rock and the 42nd President of the United States. For some reason Bill Clinton has never shown much interest in tracing his gypsy ancestry, preferring instead to track down another branch of the family that settled in Ireland.

The last King of the Kirk Yetholm gypsies, Queen Esther's son Charles Faa, was crowned in 1898. Ten thousand people turned up for the coronation on the village green, an event which had been promoted as a way of bringing economic revival to one of the poorest bits of the Borders. Photographs of the coronation show old men with wispy beards astride broken nags. The King's robes and tin crown were hired from a theatrical costumier in Edinburgh, but he still looks as if he's dressed in something run up from his granny's curtains. The gypsies, like the reivers, had become tacky heritage rather than history.

Back in the bar the conversation turned to the Clinton connection. Never one to knowingly undersell an argument, I was making the point that the presidential family was a perfect example of Borderers sticking together. Clinton's family had come from Kirk Yetholm. Hilary Roddam Clinton was from a family of Durham miners who had originated at Roddam in border Northumberland. They may have met at some American University or other but the attraction that drew them together across a crowded room obviously sprang from a niff of Border genes.

'And I suppose Monica was one of the Jedburgh Lewinskis,' said the history teacher, approaching his ten-pint target.

'I don't think Monica would have gone down well in Presbyterian Kirk Yetholm,' said I.

The bar fell about, the history teacher started to tear down the Berlin Wall again and I realized it was time I went to bed.

CHAPTER ELEVEN

Tweed Valley

T he next morning I cheated. To be honest, I couldn't face the haul out to Tuppie's Grave. So, instead, I walked the old line of the Border in the valley bottom along the Halter Burn. It was probably in the early nineteenth century that the Border shifted to the watershed a mile or so to the east. Until then the hills of Green Humbleton and Burnt Humbleton rising sharply to their respective forts were English ground.

The old and new Borders meet up by the site of an ancient chapel dedicated to the memory of St Etheldreda, daughter of an East Anglian king and wife of Egfrid, King of Northumbria in the seventh century. But Etheldreda's vocation and pledge of lifelong virginity sat unhappily with her marriage vows. As it would. For a time her husband allowed her to live in the nunnery at Coldingham in Berwickshire but, faced with a belated honeymoon, she escaped to her estates in the Fens, where she founded the cathedral at Ely. Her name also embedded itself in the English language in a most peculiar way. St Etheldreda was shortened to St Audrey, a name applied to a particular kind of tatty lace sold on her saint's day – hence tawdry meaning cheap, showy and of poor quality. She wouldn't have been amused, but by all accounts she rarely was anyway.

The Halter Burn flows into the Shotton Burn close by Yetholm Mains. It's a shifting, meandering watercourse through what in a softer, southern landscape would be called water meadows. The men who made the map obviously couldn't be doing with a burn that had a mind of its own. If it shifted left or right by a couple of feet after a flood, who knows what bother might ensue? So they taught it a lesson by removing its frontier distinction and, instead, planting a line of trees to mark the Border. So far the Shotton Burn hasn't managed to wash them away. They continue almost to the Bowmont Water, where the frontier breaks with convention and cuts across the stream at right angles. I confess I wouldn't have noticed. I confess it wouldn't have mattered if I hadn't noticed. But the meticulous Mr Logan Mack is not to be denied. He points out that this is one of only two such right-angled crossings on the whole Border, the other being at the Berwick Bounds, where the line cuts across the River Whitadder. This quirk of Border geography perhaps should have made my morning, but it didn't.

As I marched up the shoulder of Bowmont Hill I was overtaken by thoughts of irrelevance. They were sparked by that kink in the line as it crossed the Bowmont Water, a black dash on the map that matters not a jot to anybody living or dead. And I thought maybe the whole Border is irrelevant except as the setting for a colourful historical pageant. Certainly the people I'd met along the way were generally ambivalent about it. Except, of course, for the history teacher. And we couldn't take him too seriously. He was presently being collected by his wife, who was comparing his general air of wreckage after a night in the Border Hotel with the small print of the life insurance policy. Everyone else talked of the Border as if it was a quaint convention. A line drawn in impermanent diplomatic ink which had started to fade at about the same time that a Yorkshire mercenary called Guy Fawkes was planning to organize James VI and I's speedy departure from his recently acquired London Parliament – through the roof.

For the past couple of hundred years has the Border been anything more than a string of grasping and bad-tempered property disputes? Was I expecting too much from it? Where was the edginess (important word)? Where was the enduring legacy of grievance or sullen accommodation created by the memory of two great countries chafing against each other and causing sparks to fly? So far I hadn't found much of it.

There was certainly no sign of aggression on the gently undulating descents beyond Bowmont and Venchen Hills where the Border is running north-north-west, pretending not to be a Border, and where there isn't any discernible difference at all between English and Scottish ground.

That morning there had been a cartoon by Matt in the *Daily Telegraph* about the Scottish Executive's decision to ban smoking in public places. It showed a line of addicts standing on the English side of Hadrian's Wall having a fag. Leaving aside the minor point that most people living south of Lancaster probably think Hadrian's Wall is the Border, it illustrated what should have been a reawakening of the frontier's fortunes. A newly empowered Scottish Parliament promoting radically different policies should have sharpened up the line. But it seems we've become so used to our cosy, hand-knitted Border that not even the Ruritanian politics of Holyrood can generate a new interest in it. As I wandered down towards Hoselaw Mains I was tinkering with an interim conclusion that the Border really didn't matter very much at all.

But if that's the case, why were agents of one of the executive branches of government sticking pegs in the ground here?

I spotted the first of them on the verge of the Town Yetholm to Mindrum road. A little hand-painted coloured marker about twelve inches long and inscribed with the name of the Boundary Commission. Maybe the Border is still work in progress after all. The marker was obviously temporary. Easiest thing in the world to move it a yard to the east and give England an extra bit. I wondered what the penalties were for nation theft. Would anybody notice it had been moved? Would anybody care?

Two other marks have been left at the crossing of this out-of-the-way, single-track country road. The first looks unofficial but altogether bolder and more permanent than the Boundary Commission's attempt. Someone has daubed the line of the Border across the road in gold paint and six inches into England by my reckoning. The other is the DMZ between the roads departments of Northumberland and Berwickshire. I have to report that the Berwickshire tarmacadam is of an altogether higher standard than its Northumberland counterpart, but that hasn't stopped the English road men from nicking a yard of Scotland.

Just across the road is No Man's Land, an overgrown copse with a little stream called the Haggis Hall Burn running through the middle of it. It's marked on the map as a fox covert and Logan Mack says it was a particular favourite of the Border hunts. Presumably more so now that there are different hunting bans in England and Scotland. Which one would apply here? Which bobby would make the arrest – the one from Northumbria or the one from Lothian and Borders? Who would try the case – Procurator Fiscal or County Court Judge?

How this block of land has managed to evade the centuries of Border tidying and housekeeping nobody seems to know but, against the odds, it remains disputed territory. When the Robson family (no relation, at least in the last ten or fifteen generations) bought Pressen Hill farm in the 1920s, the respective councils in England and Scotland were squabbling about No Man's Land, so the new owners did the sensible thing and claimed it as their own. It's not England, not Scotland but Robson territory and that's just fine by me. It's become a place with great potential. Just imagine the things you could do here to circumvent the worst excesses of English and Scots bureaucracy. You could build a bar where people can smoke and in the beer garden behind it your customers could let off fireworks after 11 p.m. You could open a shop where you can sell apples by the pound and you could keep a horse without the need for an equine ID certificate confirming it won't poison anyone who eats it. You could even make it the venue for the target shooting events at the next British Olympics. Since 1997 handguns have been illegal in Scotland and England. The only gun users entirely unaffected by this law of course being armed robbers. Now, you may not want to do all or any of those things, but I bet you have your own selection of overbearing bureaucracy and half-digested law that you'd like to see buried in No Man's Land. I'll leave the rest of this page blank so that you can insert your own wish list.

I walked down to the farm with the present head of state, Mark Robson. On the way he pointed out several possible Borders. There was a line of trees interspersed with boulders, there was a field boundary behind the plantation and there was the Haggis Hall Burn feeding what had once been the reservoir for Pressen Mill, now landscaped as the centrepiece of an emerging wild garden. Enough options to keep the Boundary Commission in a bureaucratic frenzy for decades, he reckoned. Mr Robson wasn't at all what you'd expect from the chap running a little country sandwiched between two troublesome nations. He was welcoming, well informed and with a slightly lilting, dry sense of humour.

By the time we got to the farmhouse we were back in undisputed territory. The Border runs along the line of a wall just outside Mark Robson's back door. The farm itself is in England but, as a final gesture of independence, Mark has knocked the Border wall down so that he can park his car and his greenhouse in Scotland. When some prudent English Chancellor of the Exchequer decides to tax bedding plants, as inevitably they will, having taxed everything else, Mark Robson's ready for him.

At the end of the farm drive the Border turns sharp left and takes either to the white line down the middle of the B6396, which is my interpretation, or to the southerly roadside ditch, which is Logan Mack's. But don't let's squabble about six feet of blacktop. What we can most certainly agree about is that the highway authorities of both countries have got their road signs completely wrong. They've assumed that the Pressen Burn at the bottom of the hill is the line of the Border. It's not. So the sign welcoming drivers to 'Northumberland – England's Border Country' is in Scotland while the sign that says 'Scotland Welcomes You' is about two hundred yards premature.

At the next right-angled corner in the frontier (and we'll find a few of those in the next couple of miles) there's the start of a line of hedge that will mark the Border almost to the River Tweed. It's easy to be sniffy about hedges. In their modern form, hacked into shape by marauding agricultural flail mowers, they're much diminished. But in their full glory they have a long and colourful history. In 1552, the year they were settling the line of the Scots Dike between Sark and Esk, landowners elsewhere along the Border were being instructed that their enclosures should be 'double set with quickwood'. Two lines of thorn bushes would be planted six feet apart, with the Border line running up the middle. It's thought the idea came from the early British, who used thorn hedges as stock enclosures.

But the hedge as frontier found its most exotic expression in British Imperial India of all places. In the 1840s the East India Company began to create a hedge that ran from the Punjab by way of Delhi and Agra to the borders of modern Madhya Pradesh and Maharashtra, a total length of more than 1,500 miles. For most of its length it was a living hedge up to 10 feet high and 14 feet thick using whatever species of thorny plant would grow in a particular district. When deserts had to be crossed, hundreds of thousands of tons of harvested thorn bushes were hauled over great distances to continue the barrier. Twelve thousand men were stationed along its length in more than 1,700 guard posts. It was created as a customs hedge to maximize the revenues of the British salt tax. And it worked. It was an expensive hedge to run, costing more than a million and a half rupees a year at a time when agricultural wages were about three rupees a month. But in one year alone the salt tax collected at the hedge was twelve and a half million rupees. The great hedge of India[34] became a hated symbol of British greed and oppression. Millions died as a result of the salt tax and even the grasping imperial administration forced an occasional blush. The hedge was abandoned in the 1880s.[34]

There's nothing quite so spectacular here, as you'd expect. Just a row of ancient, contorted hawthorn. You might not give it a second glance if you didn't know this was the quickthorn frontier. You might not give it a second glance even when you do. But it has one thing in common with its Indian big brother. The salt smugglers of Berwickshire probably cursed the thorns as much as did their counterparts on the borders of the Bengal presidency.

When I walked this section of the Border with Alistair Moffat while we were making the television series, his spirits visibly lifted as we approached the Tweed. Kelso men, like certain vintages of claret, don't travel well. His dad used to call the Tweed Valley 'the inhabited world'. I'm less comfortable with it. It's too flat, too wide, too prosperous for somebody born in Liddesdale and bred in Cumberland. As you walk out on to Wark Common under giant skies you realize there's nowhere to hide. You're a pea in a floodlit drum. Making themselves scarce must have been a skill kids in the Tweed Valley learned at about the same time as they learned to walk. Because this was the way the armies came during the Anglo-Scottish wars. More dangerous, it was the way the armies retreated, hungry and vicious in defeat. They stole what they wanted and burned what was left to deny the victors the spoils. Even in what passed for peacetime the rich farmlands of Tweed were a tempting target for the wilder inhabitants of the Middle Marches.

Not that the families of the East Marches were exactly blameless. The Humes, who held sway in the Scottish East March for hundreds of years, are sometimes portrayed as the steadiest family of the Border. But, whatever you do, don't

34 Roy Moxham, *The Great Hedge of India*, Constable, 2001. A quite wonderful book.

conjure up images of their aristocratic descendant, Sir Alec Douglas Home, who was Prime Minister, ever so briefly and ever so ineffectually, and who looked like a benignly smiling skull. The old Humes had a much darker side. In 1516 a Frenchman was appointed Warden of all the Scottish Marches. According to George MacDonald Fraser in *The Steel Bonnets*, Anthony Darcy, the Sieur de la Bastie, was a thoroughly decent sort of bloke, but his appointment was an affront to the Humes. It encroached on what they regarded as their hereditary right. They tracked him to a spot near Duns, sawed off his head and took it back to Hume Castle as a trophy. If Sir Alec Douglas Home had done the same to Enoch Powell and Iain MacLeod (metaphorically speaking, of course) he might have done rather better in the 1964 general election.

Here in the East Marches property rights were always much more important than politics in deciding where the Border ran because here the land was worth having. It's some of the best agricultural land in Britain. In comparison, the disputes we came across in the Cheviots, such as the one between the Duke of Northumberland and the Douglas family, were armchair war games. The land they were fighting over was probably worth less than the lawyers' fees. It still is.

I remember once talking to the Duke of Buccleuch about his huge land holdings in the Borders (227,000 acres at the last count) and him telling me he thought people were altogether too impressed by acreages. 'What they don't understand,' he said, slightly miffed in an intensely aristocratic sort of way, 'is that an acre of mine up here is worth a great deal less than the space taken up by a waste-paper basket in an office in Canary Wharf.' It seemed a fair enough point at the time. But afterwards I tried to imagine a landscape of 227,000 waste-paper baskets. Very Tate Modern. And it didn't look anywhere near as good as the ducal estates of Dumfriesshire.

As early as the thirteenth century this bit of the Border in front of us caused an international incident and the upshot of that dispute is a seventy- or eighty-acre kink in the line. The battle of the bulge involved knights and commissioners from both countries who, needless to say, couldn't agree. So on that occasion they resorted to what they described as 'the wise men of the countryside', who set the Border on the basis of their folk memory. This is probably as good a method as any, as history seems to confirm.

One of our more recent and local creators of international Borders is a good example. Gertrude Bell, the steel magnate's daughter from the English East March, who became an advisor to the Foreign Office on Middle Eastern affairs, was a feisty lady of unshakeable conviction. But had she taken a bit more notice of the wise men of the countryside, most notably the Kurds and Marsh Arabs, when she drew the straight-line frontiers of a brand-new country called Iraq in the Arabian sands shortly after the First World War, we could have saved ourselves an awful lot of trouble.

But palm-fringed oasis this is not. The wind has got up and squally rain sweeps across the Middle Ages spread of Scotland. We're at a spot called the Duke's Strip, a reminder of a later land grab on Wark Common. It began with an Act of Parliament 'Made and passed in the thirty-seventh year of the reign of his present Majesty King George the Third, to divide, allot, and enclose the Common Moor or Tract of Waste Ground called Wark Common lying wholly or partly within the Barony or Manor of Wark in the Parish of Carham in the County of Northumberland.' To the peasantry of Wark Common it was known, more succinctly, as the robbers' charter.

The act was one of more than four thousand in the late eighteenth and early nineteenth centuries that resulted in the enclosure of almost a quarter of the productive land in England, according to the historian Eric Hobsbawm. Enclosure sprang not just from personal greed. That was used merely as the mechanism whereby a greater political end could be achieved. The commons were where the peasantry were allowed to graze their few animals. They gave the poorest of farmers a modicum of independence and that was seen as a dangerous thing. A county agricultural survey of the time made the point: 'The greatest of evils to agriculture would be to place the labourer in a state of independence. Farmers, like manufacturers, require constant labourers – men who have no other means of support than their daily labour, men whom they can depend on.' In other words, take the commons away from them and they'd be forced to accept whatever wages landowners and the new breed of factory owners chose to give them.

The new patterns of land ownership further impoverished the already poor Borders. The new entrepreneurs and agricultural capitalists saw their estates only as money machines, if they saw them at all. Many of the owners were absentee landlords. The Duke of Somerset, who owned extensive estates in Cumberland, visited them only once in sixty-six years. The money his stewards and bailiffs extracted from his tenants was exported to the south of England.

People making claims on the 2,000 or so acres up for grabs on Wark Common gathered at a meeting in Cornhill on 17 December 1798. There were representatives of the usual suspects – the Dukes of Roxburgh and Buccleuch, and a number of other local landed families hoping for a cut of the action. There were the Greys and the Comptons and the 4th Earl of Tankerville, all claiming that their ownership of bits of land in the vicinity gave them rights over the common ground. There was much talk of agricultural improvement and the social responsibility of the great men represented at the inquiry who would have the vision to drive it forward.

Great men like the 4th Earl of Tankerville, an absentee landlord who lived in Walton-on-Thames and who was described as being 'renowned for nothing but cricket playing, bruising and low company'. But he did have one notable achievement to his name. He revolutionized cricket. Until the late eighteenth century the wickets had comprised just two stumps and a single bail, but in one grudge match the Earl's gardener, 'Lumpy' Stevens, bowled four balls so accurately that they went right through the middle without disturbing the woodwork. Unfortunately those four deliveries lost the Earl a substantial bet, so to stop any such inconvenience occurring again he invented the middle stump. His invention must have been a great blessing to the cottagers of Wark Common. No doubt the comforting sound of leather on willow took the edge off the hunger pangs when the Earl of Tankerville got his portion of the enclosed common and kicked the locals off.

But I fear you're glazing over. The history of cricket can so easily have that effect now that Brian Johnston's dead. So in failing light we'd better tread on to the Redden Burn. But don't get too excited. This stream that was picked as the Border about eight hundred years ago makes the River Sark look like the Orinoco. It's a muddy dribble, so insignificant that its role has been reinforced by the building of a stretch of Border wall. Yet this was another acknowledged meeting point for the holding of truce days. I hope they got better weather.

We were caught in horizontal, icy rain the last time I was here with Alistair Moffat at the mouth of the Redden Burn where it drops into the River Tweed. That day the Border wall provided much-needed shelter. We'd arranged to meet Peter Straker Smith, who farms much of Wark Common these days and controls the fishing on the meandering Carham beat. He was going to loan us a boat and a ghillie who would row us along the Border down the middle of the Tweed.

Peter bears a striking resemblance to Clark Kent. At least he did when we'd run for cover to his centrally heated estate office and he'd spun round a couple of times to get out of a set of battered, heavy-duty tweeds that only someone reasonably well heeled would wear.

Just as an aside while Peter is struggling out of his coat, tweed cloth has precisely nothing to do with the river. The name came about because a shipping clerk inadvertently wrote tweed instead of tweel on a consignment of cloth being sent to a London tailor. Tweel is a Scottish variant of twill. The buyer thought the name tweed had marketing possibilities and it stuck.

We were warming ourselves round cups of coffee and asking the now untweeded Peter about his experience of how the Border was changing now that Scotland's Parliament had started to flex its muscles (seven stone weakling that it may be). He said that odd bits of bureaucracy were certainly changing but nothing had altered the general sweep of the way things have always been.

'The English and the Scots are both urban peoples who live a long, long way away from here. We don't matter to them. Why should we? Up to now we've lived in the middle of nowhere. I suppose the danger in the future is that we'll be living on the edge of two different nowheres.'

We chatted about the little annoyances of Border life. The snowplough crew who refused to plough across the Border but got stuck trying to turn round and were stranded for days, closing roads English and roads Scots. The body from Scotland that washed up on the English bank of the Tweed and needed a licence to be taken back across the river. The students who go to England who have to pay tuition fees and the Scottish students who don't. The really important things.

Peter's pragmatically jaundiced view of the place the Borders has in modern decision making is reflected in deep, generally forgotten history. Turn the clock back to 1375. And there's a date that hardly anybody bothers to conjure with. But in 1375, during the Hundred Years War, it was suggested by Papal negotiators, trying to broker a deal between England and France, that England should renounce its claims of territory in France in exchange for unspecified territory elsewhere. The 'unspecified' bit began with an 'S'. Don't mess with France and you can take a bite or two out of Scotland. The Borders had become an international bargaining counter and such tiddlywink politics further alienated the already disaffected locals. As we were leaving Peter said, 'Of course, the Border never makes much sense to the guy who's living on it.'

And he should know. His office lies between two of the most historically important sites on the whole of the Border line. In a field just a few hundred yards from where we'd been having our coffee, on 26 May 1018, something happened which you could argue is the reason the eastern Border ended up where it did. The battle of Carham set a marker that would eventually lead to the establishment here of a formalized frontier between two countries as yet not fully invented.

To the south King Athelstan of Wessex and his Danish successor Cnut had been putting together the building blocks of what would be England. In the north Malcolm II MacAlpin ruled a place then known as Alba but which would be the guts of Scotland. Between them was the old kingdom of Bernicia, ruled by the Earl of Bamburgh. (Yes, this is potted history which, like shrimps similarly treated, won't fill a hole for long. For a fuller, three-course description you'd better consult Alistair Moffat's cordon-bleu account of the history of the Borders which, to continue the metaphorical mix, is Titian in oils compared to my pen-and-ink cartoon.)[35]

35 Alistair Moffat, The Borders, Deerpark Press, 2002

Anyhow, put simply, Malcolm MacAlpin had struck a deal with King Owain of Strathclyde and together they marched south, intent on taking the fertile farmlands of the Tweed Valley. Eadulf, Earl of Bamburgh engaged them at Carham and his Bernician army was filleted to the last gizzard. Having had to put up with Alistair Moffat's sore feet for a fortnight while we tramped along the Border line, I feel entirely justified in making him take up the story.

Nowadays Carham is a sleepy hamlet of a dozen houses standing a hundred yards or so from a lazy bend in the meandering River Tweed. On the flat flood plain nearby, a thousand years ago, the grass was soaked with blood. Swinging their Lochaber axes, the wild Highlanders in Malcolm's host hacked the English shield-wall to pieces. Scenting slaughter and roaring their war cries, they incited each other into 'freagarrachan' or 'rage-fits' and they climbed over the wrack of dying and screaming men and drove the defeated Bernicians into the Tweed or lifted them wriggling into the air on the points of their long spears. There was no mercy on that day and the chronicler Simeon of Durham recorded the carnage when he wrote 'all the people who dwelt between Tees and Tweed were well-nigh exterminated'.

But as Alistair points out, for all the exterminating brutality of the battle at Carham, a slaughter that won Malcolm and his successors control of the Tweed Valley, they largely left the surviving farmers to their own devices. They were much more interested in maximizing the revenues of the place than in posturing as conquering heroes. They had no great knowledge of lowland farming. There was no suggestion of divvying up the good land among their own poor highlanders. It's a lesson in colonial history and nation building that Robert Mugabe would have done well to learn a thousand years later behind the borders of Zimbabwe. But Malcolm MacAlpin had the advantage of not being deranged and Swiss bank accounts hadn't yet been invented.

The other important site is the Scottish village of Birgham, lying just across the Tweed from Peter Straker Smith's office. Its name means the settlement by the bridge. Today there isn't one and there hasn't been one for more than seven hundred years. But archaeologists suspect that this was the site of the very first bridge over the lower Tweed. Built as early as the seventh century it would have been the construction wonder of Alistair's dad's inhabited world. The suspicion is that it survived into the eleventh century and it's the reason the battle of Carham happened where it did.

Yet Birgham is mainly remembered not for its civil engineering but instead for what's seen as a betrayal of Scotland's independence that was acted out at a convention held here in high summer in the year 1290. That's why in old Scottish slang the phrase 'Go to Birgham' means rather the same as 'Go to hell'.

It's said that the agreement signed that year in Birgham started the rot that led to three hundred years of Anglo-Scottish war. It could also be argued more positively (if you're not of a blinkered Scottish Nationalist persuasion) that it was in the crucible of that Birgham meeting that the political chemistry which led, eventually, to the creation of the United Kingdom began its reaction. The catalyst was a bit of rotten horsemanship.

On a stormy March night in 1286 Alexander III of Scotland set out from Edinburgh to visit his wife Yolande at Kinghorn on the north coast of the Firth of Forth. He didn't make it. His horse stumbled and he fell over a cliff at Burntisland. The man who'd tried to knock clannishness on the head and foster the idea of a Scottish kingship rooted in an honourable Celtic tradition had knocked himself on the head and inconveniently died. The heir to the Scottish throne was his only surviving grandchild, Margaret, daughter of the King of Norway. But she was just three years old and several hundreds of miles away. In the turbulent months that followed the King's death a group of guardians was appointed to try to keep order between rival claimants to the throne, the Anglo-Norman Bruces and Balliols, both linked to the Scottish king David I, both with estates in England, both one-time allies of the English Crown, neither willing to budge an inch. The guardians eventually approached Edward I of England to ask him to restore order. A treaty was drawn up confirming that Margaret, the Maid of Norway, would succeed to the throne under Edward's custody. She would also marry Edward's son, the first Prince of Wales. Naively, the Scots accepted assurances that their independence would be guaranteed, that their country would be 'separate and divided from England by its rightful boundaries, free in itself and without subjection'.

Unfortunately they didn't read the small print. When the child Margaret died on the way to her new country, King Edward began to style himself Overlord of the Land of Scotland. He insisted that all claimants to the Scottish throne should recognize him as their feudal superior. As the Commissioners sat in Birgham on the Border that day in 1290 they were putting their signatures to a document that would be quoted down the centuries as justification for Scotland's subordination.

Modern Birgham has missed a trick. At the very least the village signs should say something like 'Welcome to Birgham – the village that stuffed Scotland'. I'm sure that would attract no end of gloating English tourists, but I'm not sure what they'd find to do when they got here. There is a bar in Birgham called the Treaty, but on the day I beat a path to its door it was shut.

CHAPTER TWELVE

The River Tweed

T he Tweed is a Scottish river. It rises far to the north-
west near Moffat on the borders of Dumfriesshire,
Lanarkshire and Peeblesshire. It's run four-fifths of its
ninety-seven miles by the time it picks up the dribblings of the
Redden Burn. From here to the Bounds of Berwick it's half
Scots and half English. And then, in a final affront to its
diluted Scottishness, it surges to the sea in an English estuary.

In the fields beyond Carham Hall on the English side of the
river a bevy of mute swans is tucking into a crop of kale. In the
middle of the field a couple of them are pecking at the legs of
a scarecrow that's given up the ghost. Others are snoozing
around the compressed-air bird scarer. Today the Tweed Valley
weather is behaving itself. The trees along the riverbank are
perfectly reflected in the slow-moving water. Reflections
shattered from time to time into dancing circles by salmon
jumping in celebration of the recent end of the fishing season.
People have always marvelled at the salmon's ability to migrate
vast distances across the Atlantic and somehow find its way
back to its home river. I find it much more interesting that
they know the fishermen have packed up and gone home for
the year. On my local river, the Irt, which runs out of
Wastwater in the Lake District, you can more or less guarantee
smirking fish under Crag House Bridge the day after the
fishing ends when, for the whole of the season, they've been as
rare as hen's teeth.

Beyond the swan field the ground begins to climb through
the grassy mounds of what looks like ancient fortifications but
is in fact a kaim, a linear glacial deposit set down at the end of
the last Ice Age. The ground rises again to an ominous plug of
rock and rubble that's all that remains of the Castle of Wark. It

stands forlorn, hemmed in by bungalows and power lines, but still with a gloomy presence. Of course anything more than two storeys is positively mountainous in the Tweed Valley. As we walk towards it we pass Gallows Knoll and Gallows Hill, neither of them much bigger than the average high kerb. But when Wark was in its glory they housed a couple of the busiest production lines in the Borders. Their gibbets produced Scots corpses at a quite spectacular rate.

The reason is that Wark attracted trouble as rotten meat attracts flies. It controlled a ford on the Tweed, which in both directions was the road to the front during four centuries of Border warfare. Wark was also one of the ugliest castles in Britain. Built at the beginning of the twelfth century with the blessing of Henry I, it was a hunched, six-sided, five-storey keep. Each storey was equipped with what they described with admirable candour as 'murder holes' through which the garrison could fire, pour and hurl curses on to any besieger. They didn't have long to wait to try out their new facilities. Shortly after it was built, David I, King of Scots, attacked it three times in one year, causing much damage and managing to overpower it for a while. Until it was finally abandoned in the seventeenth century it stood in the eye of the storm, besieged and battered time and again by both Scots and English depending on who was temporarily in control.

Anybody who set up as a jobbing castle repair man in Wark in the middle of the twelfth century would, like modern plumbers, have been able to name his own price, guarantee several hundred years' work and be so much in demand that he probably refused to turn out at night or weekends. Perhaps the difficulty in getting tradesmen was the reason that in 1419 the Wark plumbing let it down. The castle, which had been overrun by the Scots, was retaken by a small group of English troops who climbed in through the sewer pipe that oozed into the Tweed.

But a hundred years later Wark was about to have a brief but scandalous golden age as one of the pivotal fortifications on the Border. It had to put up with a last, heavy-duty pounding. In 1513 James IV of Scotland invaded England because the English had invaded the French, who were Scotland's allies. He hauled along in his artillery train what was then the biggest cannon in Christendom, Mons Meg. It thundered holes out of Wark big enough to be acts of God.

But a few weeks later there was Flodden and King James was dead; long live the new King James. And then there was the battle of Solway Moss, which broke the new King James's heart. His troops were humiliated. It's said that only twenty of his soldiers were killed in action but that hundreds were drowned in the Solway marshes and those that survived were stripped to their stockings not by the victorious English army but by Scottish reivers who picked through them as if they were walking corpses.

When James V turned his face to the wall and wept and raged himself to death, Scotland found itself ruled from a cradle by a baby girl whom he had called Maddy and we call Mary, Queen of Scots.

Henry VIII had Scotland at his feet, but for the moment he chose not to trample. The great proponent of marriage, just about to embark on his sixth, saw the chance to have England and Scotland united under one ruler. He would have his son Edward betrothed to the baby Queen. The Scots quibbled and Henry snapped. He unleashed a reign of terror unmatched by any English ruler before or since. Longshanks, the Hammer of the Scots, would have been shocked. Queen Victoria, in whose name some of the most grotesque abuses were perpetrated in the vain attempt to subdue the Empire, would have been dispirited.

Wark was one of the jumping-off points for the bloodshed that became known as 'the Rough Wooing'.

It began routinely enough with a spot of orchestrated civil war among the Border families. Nothing new in that. Both countries had used the technique often enough before. They would take some festering local dispute and harness it to the rickety cart of national policy. Scottish families would be persuaded by bribe and the blind eye of Border law to cause trouble in England's interest. At the same time English families would be in the pay of the Scottish King. For decades nobody in the Borders dare shake another man's hand. The man you drank with tonight could be a sworn enemy tomorrow. The enemy you fought tomorrow could be standing shoulder to shoulder with you in a week's time. And a week was a bloody long time in Border politics.

In 1543 Sir Thomas Wharton, the consummate English Warden, had the Armstrongs and Elliots, Nixons and Storeys pillaging hither and thither in the Scottish Borders on King Henry's behalf. If he thought they were slacking he would descend with Cumbrian riders to burn out farms in Armstrong and Elliot territory. The anarchy spread to the Middle and East Marches. Pringles and Robsons, Rutherfords and Davidsons were all drawn into the web of gratuitous violence. The Border was ablaze from end to end. There were hundreds if not thousands of raids which reduced what remained of the settled population of the Border counties to new extremes of poverty and fear.

But this was only the start. In 1544 King Henry appointed Edward Seymour, Earl of Hertford to intensify the campaign. He was going to teach Scotland a lesson it wouldn't soon forget. He landed an army at Leith which was reinforced by some thousands of Borderers, mainly Scots, and which burned and murdered its way from Holyrood to Berwick. Edinburgh was devastated, Dunbar destroyed. Men of fighting age were killed. Women and children weren't spared. In sloppy modern phraseology it would probably be called genocide.

But bad as the damage inflicted by Hertford's mercenary army was, in the Borders things were even worse. The father and son Wardens of the English Middle and East Marches, Lord William and Sir Ralph Eure, turned a great swathe of the Borders into ash and rubble. From Wark they attacked Kelso and Jedburgh, burning what they could and pulling down what they couldn't. Village after village, farm after farm was put to the torch and if the people and the livestock were still in the buildings hard luck. King Henry was delighted and composed 'some pretty music' to celebrate. But, on reflection, he didn't think his wardens had been quite brutal enough. So, 3,000 mercenaries drawn from just about every country in Europe were sent as reinforcements. Spanish and Greek and Irish soldiers of fortune hacked their way through the Borders the following year. There were terrible abuses and from a wide sweep of the Borderlands any of the population left standing fled.

By the end of 1545 the view north from Wark's battlements was of an empty land with smoke on the horizon.

King Henry read his reports from the front and saw they were good. But the riding families also saw an opportunity, particularly when Scotland began to fight back. So long as the wars lasted they could make a living, paid by England one day and Scotland the next. Sometimes, on the really good days, by both on the same. The focus on survival and the easy resort to revenge hardened their souls. Civilization had been unravelled and they picked up the blood-stained threads and wove them into a sampler of hideous normality.

But Wark is remembered for its part in this monstrous time hardly at all. Instead, its lasting memorial is a tale of gallantry involving a courteous king and a beautiful lady which the battle-hardened garrison at Wark would have thought was total baloney and which really needs a Pre-Raphaelite painting to do it justice. The story goes that Edward III attended a ball at Wark in 1348. His hostess was the temptingly beautiful Joan Plantagenet, the Fair Maid of Kent, who eventually married the Black Prince and was mother to Richard II. But her husband at the time was the Earl of Salisbury, the owner of Wark. (Actually he wasn't her husband, according to a Papal Bull issued by Pope Clement VI the following year which ruled that she was already married to someone else – but try to keep up.)

Anyhow, during the dancing, the Countess lost a garter. King Edward picked it up and saw a group of courtiers snigger either at the Fair Maid's embarrassment or, more likely, because he was widely rumoured to have tried to tempt the lady into the royal bed on more than one occasion. With a royal flourish he put the jewelled decoration on his own leg and ticked off the sniggerers: 'Honi soit qui mal y pense,' says he – evil be to him who evil thinks. And so was founded the most senior and the oldest order of British chivalry, the name of which I've quite forgotten. It's also claimed that the incident happened at the battle of Crécy, in Calais and at Windsor Castle, but as we're at Wark let's give this poor battered spot its brief moment of heraldic grandeur. For goodness' sake Wark needs something to take its mind off the blood on the walls and the guts on the floor.

I climbed out on to the rubble heap and played king of the castle. For a few minutes I was master of all I surveyed along the Tweed. In the village of Wark, huddled round my feet, nothing stirred. It was as if everyone had taken cover in anticipation of yet another siege. But it occurred to me at that moment that it might be something more serious. I remembered that in all the times I've driven through Wark I've never seen a soul. Maybe they were all killed in 1513 and the village is a sham to convince the Scots the place is still defended. Perhaps somebody in authority has decided that Wark is still too dangerous for habitation.

Then I found a bit of evidence that supported the lingering danger theory. As I was leaving, I spotted a sign put up by English Heritage saying that you shouldn't go anywhere near the castle because it may be dangerous. Good job the bureaucrats of English Heritage weren't around in 1513. Just imagine the industrial tribunal claim of the people on the receiving end of Mons Meg. Fortunately in the sixteenth century there weren't solicitors' agents lurking about at troublespots like Wark and sidling up to soldiers from the garrison. 'Have you by any chance tripped over a dead Scotsman? That cleft in your head – could your commanding officer have prevented it by not exposing you to the obvious danger of taking part in a siege? As you appear to have no ears or nose, were you made aware of your rights under schedule three of the Mercenary Troops Prevention of Accidental Injuries Bill? No win, no fee, of course.'

There would have been no takers, because no win, no fee was the terms they worked under anyway. They didn't need anyone to tell them their rights. They all knew well enough that they didn't have any if they ended up on the losing side, which is why the Borderers were so adept at spotting winners. As a Bishop of Durham once put it, they went into battle with their badges very lightly sewn on. In their eyes Divine Right had nothing to do with kings of either persuasion. It was the right of the Borderer to hold his ground.

CHAPTER THIRTEEN

Coldstream Bridge

T he Tweed takes a great sweeping loop by way of Cornhill on the English side to Coldstream on the Scots. Just where the loop begins a little classical temple stands on the Scottish bank in the grounds of the Lees estate. The one-time owners of the great house at Lees provide a vignette of how even the most troublesome of the Border families managed to live down their past and prosper. By the time they started building on the banks of the Tweed the family were known by the name Marjoribanks, pronounced Marchbanks. The name originates as a memory of Lady Marjorie, the daughter of King Robert the Bruce, who held lands in Dumfriesshire. All very grand.

But they started out as bad old Johnstones, one of the scourge families of the Scottish West March. When they came second here to the more enduring Maxwells (enduring in the same sense as emphysema and chronic back pain), some of the brighter young Johnstones headed for Edinburgh in search of peace and fortune. They started with a modest wine and fish merchant's business but soon progressed to adventure and wealth with the East India Company. A string of them were Deputy Governors of the Bank of Scotland; some were partners and one Chairman of Coutts bank. Others were Members of Parliament, industrialists, brewers and shipping magnates.

But the family didn't quite manage to shake off its earlier rough edges. Two of them died on the ill-fated Darien expedition, a reiverly rash attempt to set up a Scottish trading outpost on the isthmus of Darien near Panama at the end of the seventeenth century. They still meddled in dangerous politics. A Marjoribanks was secretary and intelligence officer to the Jacobite Old Pretender in Cadiz. Another with suspected Jacobite leanings was Edward, who has been described as having 'a violent and excitable temper, amounting almost to madness at times, so that he had to be physically restrained'.[36] You can imagine him looking out from a tower in Dumfriesshire and raging about the iniquities of the Maxwells. Yet another has been branded 'grave and harsh'. Perfect reiver material. One of them, raised to the peerage as Lord Marjoribanks, was run over a week later by a horse-drawn bus outside his Newcastle club. The Johnstones always were accident prone. And when the family and the house at Lees fell on hard times, in an echo of the wild reiving days, the mansion was burned down by a raiding party from the Scottish Border fire brigade as a training exercise.

But the reason I stopped across the river from the Lees wasn't to tell you the story of the Johnstones turned Marjoribankses at all. That's just another fit of digression. It was that at this point there's a most peculiar kink in the Border, unlike anything to be found along the seventeen miles in which the Tweed is the frontier line from the Redden Burn to the Berwick Bounds. The Border abandons the centre line of the river and takes to dry land on the English side, leaving half a field south of the water in Scotland. Logan Mack reported a theory that the Tweed had shifted its course here yet could find no evidence of it. But it seems this area, when it was common ground, was called Dry Tweed, which could give at least some slender credence to the idea. On Armstrong's 1769 map of Northumberland it's called the Scotch Haugh, so it's fair to assume that for at least 250 years it's been a part of Scotland. But its local name is simpler, to the point and carrying clues to tradition if not to truth. It's called the Baa' Green and the story goes that its nationality

36 Roger Marjoribanks, Marjoribanks Journal No. 3, 1996

was decided by a Scottish victory in a football match (actually probably a handball game) against England.

But that was more than two hundred and fifty years ago and, as I don't have John Motson's statistical database to hand, I'm afraid I can't tell you if that was the last time Scotland managed such a result. Having, on occasion, seen them play football in recent years, probably.

While offence is in the air and as I stroll down to Cornhill, this is perhaps the moment to own up to the great heresy. I think the Tweed, by the time we reach it on this journey, can be a bit tedious in parts. Flotillas of salmon fishers marshalled by fearsome ghillies armed to the teeth with gaffs are probably mustering below Coldstream bridge as I speak to impress on me the error of my ways. But as the unspeakable has been spoken I'd better make a shot at defending the position. By now the Tweed is a broad, slow, lazy river. A couch potato of a river. It lolls and sighs as if everything is just too much bother for it. Even when it comes to weirs and rapids it takes a deep breath and sucks its teeth like a tradesman who's about to tell you the job can't be done except at a monstrous price. And then even that's too much trouble and it goes back to sleep, snoring its way past pillowed islands to the deep cradle of the sea.

For drama it's not a patch on the Duddon or Liddel.

There, I've said it.

Now admittedly I've never seen the Tweed with its dander up, when it rises ten or twelve feet and carries everything before it like a broad-chested diva advancing to her curtain call. Maybe I'd be more impressed if I had. And there are pretty views on the Tweed, to be sure. Carham church framed by trees and a somnolent bend in the river and the majestic bridge over the cold stream designed by Smeaton, who built the Eddystone lighthouse, standing with its hands on its hips and its legs planted firmly apart in the rolling brown grey water and challenging the river to do its worst. But best of all, when I get to Coldstream bridge there's nobody there. The fishers must be lying in wait for me further downstream.

In fact the only fisherman in sight was a heron waiting under the bridge for its supper. Somebody, and I can't remember who, once memorably described the heron as a flamingo in clerical grey. The Presbyterian bird rose with dripping feet and seemed to stall before idly flapping away up river. When Alistair Moffat and I were walking the Border he stopped off in Cornhill to hear about the religious differences that persist between England and Scotland. A more democratic Presbyterianism in Scotland with its simple, some would say dour orders of service. A system that put ecclesiastical decision making in the hands of the burgeoning Scottish middle classes. In England a hierarchical, costumed Anglicanism owing allegiance to bishops and the establishment. The differences are still there, but the seemingly universal rise and rise of the fundamentalist happy clappies who recognize only one Border, one with its ultimate customs post at the pearly gates, will no doubt blur the distinctions in time.

But once, religious turf wars were a pivotal influence on the firming up of notions of a Scottish state and therefore central to the hardening of the Border itself. In the twelfth century there were attempts to undermine the territorial claims of the archbishopric of York in southern Scotland and to diminish the power of the Glasgow-based parish of St Kentigern in northern England. Even the most powerful of the northern saints, Cuthbert, lost lands in Lothian to the Church of St Andrews. Henry I's establishment of the priory of St Mary in Carlisle (the forerunner of Carlisle cathedral) was designed to give a south-facing focus to religious life in the English Cumbria created by William Rufus.

What kings couldn't do, however, was break the bond between the people of the Borders and their favourite Celtic saints. Kentigern, Ninian, Cuthbert and Oswald all retained a following that refused to be limited by any political frontier, and expansionist Scottish kings like David I realized that these loyalties could be harnessed to their cause. The old saints were done up in a new costume of religious orthodoxy. David encouraged religious houses with English roots to establish in Scotland – the Augustinians in Jedburgh and Holyrood, the Tironensian order in Selkirk. And it wasn't a one-way traffic. The abbey at Holm Cultram in Cumberland was an offshoot of Melrose Abbey and the priory at Canonbie south of the Rufus frontier was a cell of Jedburgh. When King David said his prayers he knew he'd invested enough in religious expansion to be able to sneak in the odd request for divine intervention in support of his political ambitions as well.

I walked on into Scotland. High above the Border line, in the centre of one of the parapets of Coldstream bridge, there's a plaque commemorating the poet Robert Burns' first crossing into England on 7 May 1787.

O Scotia my dear my native soil
For whom my warmest wish to heaven is sent
Long may thy hardy sons of rustic toil
Be blest with health and peace and sweet content.

A strangely anodyne verse to pick as celebration of a man who saw the English-dominated Border as an accursed reminder of the destruction of Scottish independence. A man who only seven years later was threatened with the charge of sedition. I think these lines would be more appropriate:

Fareweel to a' our Scotish fame,
Fareweel our ancient glory;
Fareweel even to the Scotish name,
Sae fam'd in martial story!
Now Sark rins o'er the Solway sands,
And Tweed rins to the ocean,
To mark whare England's province stands,
Such a parcel of rogues in a nation!

Coldstream was used to rogues. Before the bridge was built it stood by a ford of the Tweed. When the river was in spate and crossings couldn't be made, it became a crowded, not-a-room-to-be-had-for-love-nor-money Scotch frontier town. It hummed with gossip and was enlivened by the scurryings of rats and spies. It became one of the main listening posts on the Border. In its ale houses and alleyways titbits of rumour would be exchanged and paid for. Feuds would be reported, alliances hinted at. The position of advancing armies would be plotted on beer-swilled tables. Edward I on his way to the slaying of Berwick, Hertford's brutal foreplay ahead of the Rough Wooing.

And then in the bitter winter of 1659 there were whispers of the approach of another force, this time from the north. It was led by General George Monck, the Parliamentary military commander in Scotland who had commanded the infantry at Cromwell's victory at the battle of Dunbar and who brutally suppressed opposition to the Protectorate in Stirling and Aberdeen and Dundee. But Cromwell was now dead and his son, Richard, was no Lord Protector. News was ferried across the Tweed of the threat of civil unrest in London and that an army faction had overthrown the Rump Parliament. By Hogmanay the river had subsided enough to allow the army to cross and on New Year's Day 1660 Monck's Regiment of Foote splashed into England. In five weeks they were in London; by

April Monck had persuaded the army to allow a free Parliament. One of its first acts was to vote for the return of the monarchy. On 25 May 1660 Charles II landed at Dover. On the way to London and his coronation the King to be conferred on Monck the Order of the Garter, which became the basis of the cap badge of the oldest serving regiment of the British Army. From an uncomfortable December billet in an obscure little town on the Border they took the name the Coldstream Guards.

As for Monck himself, he found that falling into the ways of the Borderers and changing sides did him no end of good. He was created Duke of Albemarle and made Captain General of the army and Master of the King's Horse. During the Great Plague of 1665 and the Great Fire of 1666 he governed London.

Just along the street from the house in Coldstream where Monck had his headquarters I stopped for a drink in what turned out to be a Presbyterian sort of pub where there was a dour lack of service. The regulars had a shifty look to them as if I was the man from the social. Either that or they were expecting another visit from the Earl of Hertford. When I'd convinced a chap at the bar that I wasn't the scouting party for an English invasion, nor yet even remotely interested in the veracity of the forms he'd filled in to get his giro, he accepted a drink. By rubbing his empty glass he managed to conjure up a barman in rather the same way that Aladdin brought the genie out of the lamp. Unfortunately, unlike the genie, the barman only had one wish and that was for his shift to end.

Fuelled with a free pint, the giro man perked up a bit.

'S'aathesame,' was his response to my casual enquiry about whether or not there was much of a difference between people in Coldstream and people in Cornhill on the other side of the Border river.

'Sept'enrugbysoan.' I gathered that the English fans from Cornhill get safe passage into the pubs of Coldstream on international days, presumably to act out in ritualized form the bauchling and finger jabbing that would have led to the real thing on earlier days of truce.

'Usetaehaetaedrink'nEngland.' And here was a proper difference between the nations, even though it, too, has now been swept away. In the bad old days – and we're talking the late twentieth century here – pubs in Scotland closed earlier than those in England. On Sunday pubs north of the Border didn't open at all. So at Scottish closing time and on the Sabbath, Coldstream drinkers would, like the reivers before them, head across the river to lift what they could in the shortest possible time. In this case as many glasses as they could in the extra hour of drinking time. But, like reiving, cross-Border drinking was governed by arcane rules too. Particularly on a Sunday. Drinkers were supposed to be bona fide travellers and a quick flick across Coldstream bridge and back didn't count, so the Lord Wardens (sorry, the constabulary) would insist that drinkers took a ten-mile detour home by way of the next bridge up the river at Kelso.

Giro man and the bartender slipped back into the silence of the vault, so I claimed to be a bona fide traveller and escaped.

There was marginally more life in the old graveyard at Lennel, the setting of which has been much enhanced by the building next door of a waste water treatment works by East of Scotland Water. But it was a golden, generous afternoon and I sat for a while among the leaning gravestones and watched a young rabbit explore the world. Maybe it was a descendant of one of the most famous of all literary rabbits, because Beatrix Potter used to take her holidays at Lennel House just along the road on the way out from Coldstream. She sat in the garden and made up her stories and painted mushrooms.

The church at Lennel, dedicated to St Mary by the Bishop of St Andrews in 1243, is a ruin now. Only its ivy-covered west gable points shakily at the clear sky. But this was the convent that Sir Walter Scott's Marmion visited on the eve of the battle of Flodden, which took place just four or five miles away across the Tweed. Scott was another regular visitor to Lennel House. What a pity he and Beatrix Potter didn't coincide. She could have lightened up the Waverley novels no end and he could have made Mr MacGregor, the gardener, more believably fearsome.

As peaceful as it seems on such an afternoon, Lennel church had a dark reputation. In the early nineteenth century the lonely graveyard here was a target for Resurrectionists, body snatchers who supplied corpses for the surgeons of Edinburgh. There are still a couple of mort safes in the graveyard, padlocked iron grave covers weighing more than a ton to keep the dead out of the clutches of the living.

And the story's told of one local worthy who would have been more than a match for the grave robbers.[37] We're not given his full name, just that Jamie S. was a drinker (I hope not in the pub I've just left) and that he would stumble home each night past Lennel churchyard. A gang of Coldstream lads lay in wait for him one night and as he passed rose, one after the other, moaning and draped in sheets. He ignored the first few but when he drew level with the last said to the spectre, 'Noo, then! Is this a gineral resurrection, or is yan or twa ev ye just having a quiet daunder by yersels?' They caused him no further trouble and eventually he joined the queue for resurrection's Checkpoint Charlie in the same churchyard.

Bodies and religious frontiers are to be a recurring theme along this section of the Border. A mile or so to the north-east

37 Edmund Bogg, *A Thousand Miles of Wandering in the Border Country*, Mawson, Swan and Morgan, Newcastle, 1898

on the English side of the river and just before it picks up the waters of its only proper English tributary, the River Till, in the middle of a cornfield is the roofless ruin of what's called St Cuthbert's chapel. In later years this was the private chapel of the Lords of Tillmouth, but more important to our story is that it's said to be one of the many places where the saint's body rested on the long and convoluted journey from Holy Island to the shrine at Durham as his monks carried Cuthbert's remains to safety in the face of Viking attacks on the north-east coast. But this bit of the trip was relatively easy-going. They floated him down the river from Melrose in a stone coffin. And if you don't believe me you'll surely believe Sir Walter Scott:

> From sea to sea, from shore to shore,
> Seven years Saint Cuthbert's corpse they bore
> They rested them in fair Melrose,
> But though alive he loved it well
> Not there his relics might repose,
> For, wondrous tale to tell,
> In his stone coffin forth he glides,
> A ponderous bark for river tides,
> Yet light as gossamer it glides
> Downward to Tillmouth cell.[38]

And before you write that story off as superstitious hooey on a par with supposed relics of the True Cross, which, if laid end to end, would have made something the size of the Empire State Building, you should know that a ten-foot-long stone coffin was discovered at St Cuthbert's chapel. It isn't there any more because a local farmer tried to turn it into a

38 Sir Walter Scott, *Marmion*, Ballantyne, 1808

cattle trough. The next morning he found it rent asunder – or at least broken.

At the mouth of the River Till where it runs into the Tweed we're standing on a religious as well as political front line. The saints came marching into the argument about where the Border should be set, too. The great religious houses at places like Melrose and Jedburgh had become rich and powerful by the grant of lands from kings anxious to tidy up their souls before they went. Saints like Aidan and Ninian had a following that monarchs and would-be monarchs ignored at their peril. And the most powerful of them all was Cuthbert. From his shrine in Europe's greatest Romanesque church at Durham, Cuthbert's glow spread from Yorkshire almost to Edinburgh. His bishops were made princes and wielded temporal as well as spiritual power.

When the English army, led by Thomas Howard, Earl of Surrey (and soon to be Duke of Norfolk and Earl Marshal of England), massed on the eve of the battle of Flodden, above it fluttered the flags of two saints, St Etheldreda, whose acquaintance we made outside Yetholm, and St Cuthbert. Apparently neither were choosy about the company they kept because the army they blessed was a real ragbag of villainy, most notably the contingent from the West and Middle Marches brought by Lord Dacre. Here assembled were the floor sweepings of Gilsland and Tynedale, Alston and Eskdale. It was a scratch army because Henry VIII's main force was campaigning with considerable success in France. In an attempt to make the English cut short their French war, the Queen of France had written to James IV of Scotland, which had a mutual defence treaty with France, asking him to 'advance three feet onto English ground'.

In late August 1513, ignoring portents that told of a Scottish defeat, he went rather more than a yard. At the head of the largest army Scotland ever mustered – some say 100,000 men but it was probably less than half that – he crossed the Border at the Coldstream ford and took the castles at Norham and Wark, Ford, Etal, Duddo and Chillingham. His advance seemed unstoppable. But then King James spent a few days fiddling with Lady Heron's underwear at Ford Castle and a chunk of his army deserted.

In keeping with the chivalrous practice of the time, Surrey sent a messenger inviting King James to meet him in battle on 9 September. On the day, the Scots forces took up seemingly impregnable positions on Flodden Ridge and refused to budge. So 'the auld crooked Earl', as James dismissively described his opponent, sent his much smaller force on a route march through the mists and drizzles of that autumn afternoon. He lined up his troops between James and Scotland. The King was tempted from the ridge. The breeze was in his favour, so he set fires on the ridge and under cover of the smoke marched down the hill. James, on foot, marched at their head. By the time the armies could see each other they were just a few pike lengths apart. It was the last battle in which English bowmen played a significant part and the first in which artillery played a pivotal role. Flodden was a clash of technologies. The lighter English field artillery was more manoeuvrable than the cumbersome Belgian guns used by the Scots. The shafts of the seventeen-and-a-half-foot Scotch pikes, so effective in defence against cavalry charge, were hacked to pieces by the billheads of the English halberds. As dusk crept over them, reiver fought reiver in blood-streaming hand-to-hand combat. Cumberland riders harried and cut down their Scots neighbours. At the final darkness 10,000 Scots were dead compared with 1,500 English. Among the mounded corpses were the tangled remains of most of the Scottish aristocracy and the body of a King.

The reivers left standing then went back to their day job. They stripped and robbed the dead. They pursued the wounded survivors and robbed them too. Flodden is portrayed as a clash of nationalities: the revenge for Bannockburn. Implied in these descriptions is that the people fighting on Flodden Field were participants in a patriotic war. But the concept of the national interest came a poor second to concerns for their own welfare and loyalty to family and place. And the families in question were neither Stuart nor Tudor, the places neither England nor Scotland. Reivers from Tynedale harried the baggage train of the battered and hungry English army, stole their horses and took prisoners whom they handed over to the Scots. It was said at the time by a Bishop of Durham that English Borderers 'have doon more harm at this tyme to our folks than the Scottes dyd'.

In the weeks following the battle, stories began to circulate in the Borders of strange happenings that had predicted the Scottish calamity. It was reported that an old man, the double of Merlin the wizard, had appeared before King James at his prayers in the palace at Linlithgow as his army was assembling and warned him that if he didn't abandon his campaign, disaster would follow. A spectral herald had stood at Edinburgh's Mercat Cross in the dead of night, so they said, and read a roll-call of the Scots gentry who would appear before his master in the other world. It was the roll-call of those who fell at Flodden two weeks later.

These were stories to send a shiver through the hardest of the Redesdale or Bewcastle men. Because, for all his brazen exterior, the Borderer was deeply superstitious. In his world evil spirits had to be discouraged from creeping under the eaves, hobgoblins haunted woodland glades and the evil eye was hopefully blinded by the presence of an army of saints. Whether riding or at war, at enchanted places or by holy wells they would ask for a blessing on their enterprises, however criminal or barbaric those may have been.

Just such a place can be found a short way from Flodden Field, by the rainbow-arched bridge across the River Till at Twizel. It was the bridge crossed by forces of the Earl of Surrey as he outflanked the Scots army in the hours before the battle. St Helen's Well, mentioned in Scott's *Marmion*, is named for Helena, the mother of the Roman Emperor Constantine the Great. One version of her life is that she was the daughter of a British king taken as a concubine by Constantine's father, Constantius Chlorus, when he was serving with the Roman army at York. But her fame as a devout Christian patron was inspired by her mission to save the sites of the Holy Land. Around AD 320 she built the Church of the Nativity at Bethlehem and the Church of the Holy Sepulchre in Jerusalem. She organized excavations of the holy places and her workmen discovered the remains of the True Cross. (Which teaches me a lesson for being sniffy about it earlier.)

And St Helen's Well would have been a firm favourite of the Border families for two reasons. First of all she was the very saint to evoke if you wanted to find things that were lost – cattle were a particular speciality. And when she was unearthing the True Cross she also found the cross on which St Dimas was crucified. If you're not on nodding acquaintance with him, he was the old thief who repented on Calvary but who, as a young man, had given shelter to the Holy Family on their flight into Egypt. But even better than that, he was a reiver himself who robbed and pillaged and rustled livestock across the borders of Egypt and Judaea.

'Saint Helen and Saint Dimas make the Redesdale cattle fat and the hot trod slow.'

CHAPTER FOURTEEN

Ladykirk Church

The valley of the Till with its overhanging, water-worn cliffs festooned in tumbling ivy is a lovely spot. Swans nest on the islands at its mouth and the river is said to produce the finest, maddest pike in all the Borders. Brooding over the scene is a cliff-top ruin where, seventeen years before Flodden, national politics had exploded on the Border. In 1496 James IV invaded England in support of Perkin Warbeck, who claimed he had been one of the Princes in the Tower and therefore the rightful heir to the throne of Richard III. Warbeck was actually the son of a clerk from Tournai, which didn't make him a bad person but did leave his monarchical ambitions a bit threadbare. For sheer nerve he certainly ended up in the aristocracy of frauds and chancers. But his brass neck wasn't enough to save him. It succumbed to a rope necklace at the end of it all.

But in the twilight of the fifteenth century it suited France and Scotland very well to back even the daftest of claims if it served to loosen the English Crown. They rose in support of the Warbeck plot to overthrow Henry Tudor, upstart founder of the Tudor dynasty who, after Richard's death at Bosworth, had claimed the throne as Henry VII by reason of his being the grandson of Henry V's widow, Katherine of Valois. I hope you're concentrating because at the end of this chapter there's going to be a test.

But back to the ruin. Twizel Castle, high above the Till, was the first place to be destroyed by James during the campaign that failed to dislodge Henry VII. But the Twizel raid did have an enduring effect. To try to discourage King James from further silly adventures on his northern frontier Henry VII proposed a marriage between his daughter, Margaret Tudor, and the Scottish King. It took place in 1503 and one hundred years later was the basis of James VI's claim to the English throne on the death of Elizabeth. The Union of the Crowns started here.

You can still see bits of the original Twizel Castle among the ruins on the cliff, but most of what's there now are the remains of a vast gothick folly commissioned at the end of the eighteenth century by a political writer called Sir Francis Blake. A castle with hundreds of rooms, standing to five storeys with round towers at each corner and never finished. Building went on for more than half a century and the cost drove Blake to the point of bankruptcy. Pursued by his creditors, it's said he had to seek sanctuary in the Abbey at Holyrood for a while, which must have been a bit galling for a man who, in his earlier political career, had written pamphlets about how the country should manage the national debt. On the other hand, perhaps he would have been perfect Chancellor of the Exchequer material.

I whistled along the Tweed past the low, scrubby mounds of Dreeper and Kippie Islands (both English, according to the map) and arrived at the handsome Ladykirk and Norham bridge. It was given the nickname Checkpoint Jimmy by the *Guardian* newspaper in the run-up to the first elections for the Scottish Parliament in 1999.

As Scotland debates differential income tax, it is perfectly possible to conceive, even without full independence, a future with higher excise taxes on one side of this bridge. Jim Sheppard, the newsagent in Norham, could make his fortune if English cigarettes were cheaper. If it were the other way round, he could be ruined.[39]

By such important issues could the new Border with a semi-independent Scotland be defined. But there were other little practicalities that would continue to make the Border osmotic. The Scottish residents of Ladykirk wanted a new sub-post

39 *The Guardian*, 20 April 1999

office but had to get permission from a chap in Gateshead. Postcodes strayed across the line and Border Television, with the most popular local television news service in Britain, covered the English and Scottish Border counties.

Guardian reporter Matthew Engel was interested by the obvious lack of nationalism he discovered on both sides of the Norham bridge.

The sparsely populated communities of north Northumberland don't feel intensely English, since they know London thinks damn all of them. Some people even support Scotland at sport, which would be unthinkable in reverse. The nearby Scottish towns are largely sufficient unto themselves. They have to be, because the road links are wretched and the railways non-existent. The inhabitants are as suspicious of Glasgow and Edinburgh as they are of London . . . If Glaswegians are 90-minute Nats, caring for Scotland only when the football is on, Borderers appear to be 80-minute Nats – the duration of a rugby match.

His conclusion about what he described as a thin and whimsical Border was 'Politics in these parts has probably not really been passionate since the battle of Flodden, 1531.'

Well, we couldn't expect to get through three paragraphs without a *Guardian* typo, could we? I walked up to Ladykirk where, thirty-one years before Flodden if you believe the *Guardian*, or thirteen years if you believe every other document of record, the building of a church began on the orders of James IV.

Because of Flodden James is remembered as a loser, rash and probably stupid. In fact he was dashing and talented, a patron of the arts and education. Scotland had three universities during his reign. England had only two. His interests ranged from music, poetry and theatre to dentistry and golf. (Everybody's allowed one flaw in their character.) His greatest wish was to lead a crusade and he was dedicated to the ideals of Arthurian chivalry. Crusading wasn't possible. The squabbling and plotting Scottish nobility made sure of that. The chances were that James wouldn't have had a throne when he got back. So he took the safer option and campaigned chivalrously through the bedrooms of Scotland. By the time the marriage to Margaret Tudor was suggested he already had five illegitimate children and a pregnant live-in mistress, Lady Margaret Drummond. But in 1502 she was poisoned. The suspicion was that Scots promoters of the dynastic marriage feared Henry VII would hear about the lady James had moved into his Linlithgow Palace and back out of the arrangement. The King was distraught. It was the second great tragedy of his life.

The first happened when he was just fifteen years old and should have forewarned him about the danger of messing with Borderers. Two of the most devious of the Border families, the Humes and the Hepburns, encouraged him to lead a campaign against his father, James III. Young James had been told by the rebels that his father would be kept safe, that all they wanted was his abdication because his unpopularity was threatening to cause civil unrest in Scotland. The uprising came to a head at the battle of Sauchieburn near Stirling in 1488. The old king was thrown from his horse and badly injured. He called for a priest, who promptly finished him off. The penance young James did for the part he'd played in his father's death almost finished him off too.

While crossing the Norham ford in 1500, his horse stumbled and he fell into a fishing steill, a deep pool in which salmon fishers cast their nets. Weighed down by the heavy iron penance chain he always wore round his waist and to which he added a new link each year, he almost drowned. He believed he was saved by the direct intervention of the Virgin

Mary and in thanks he ordered the building of the Kirk of Our Lady of the Steill. It was built to last, forty feet above the river to keep it safe from flood and with the roof and even the pews made of stone to protect it from fire. But just to make doubly certain, a notice behind the church door announces that these days it's insured with Norwich Union.

It was in the Ladykirk that the last formal peace treaty between England and Scotland was signed in 1559. The Treaty of Chateau Cambresis signed in Flanders in April that year is evidence of how events on the England–Scotland Border wormed their way to the very heart of European politics. The main treaty ended sixty-five years of war between the Habsburgs and the Bourbons, France and Spain, for the control of Italy. But one of the clauses in the settlement henceforth prohibited Queen Elizabeth of England from any acts of aggression within Scotland. On 4 August 1559 English and Scots Commissioners gathered at the Ladykirk altar to ratify the peace. Not that there would be much of that for another eighty years. Just less official war.

Architecturally the church is Scotch Gothic, which is a bit like ordinary Gothic with cellulite. The buttresses look as if they're about to bend under the weight of the stone-slabbed roof. But that's not to say Ladykirk is without its charms. Its grey gloomy interior under a soaring stone vault would be the perfect setting for the final showdown of a Harry Potter movie. But the whole place would be immeasurably improved if a bolt of lightning took down William Adam's absurd round-topped tower. You have to wonder if Adam had ever seen Ladykirk before he did his drawings. Maybe there's a Georgian church somewhere in Edinburgh with a Scotch Gothic tower. Whatever the reason, the one at Ladykirk stands as proof that even the greatest architectural dynasties occasionally cobble a design together on the back of a fag packet when they've got behind with the grocery bills.

I sat by the church on an old grave slab patterned grey and orange with lichen and looked along the river, imagining the royal patron of Ladykirk riding up from the ford on one of his visits to inspect the building's progress. Handing out 'drinksilver' to the masons and quarrymen, complimenting 'Thomas Peblis, glas wricht' on his work, for which James had shelled out the princely sum of £67. Expensive glasswork was obviously rare enough to merit specific comment so close to a frontier where stone throwing, literal and metaphorical, was commonplace. The labours at Ladykirk went on for many years. The church still wasn't finished in 1513. On his last crossing of the Norham ford on the way to Flodden James would have seen it on the skyline. As he felt the heavy chain at his waist he no doubt hoped he'd done enough to merit continued divine support. But on that occasion St Cuthbert was calling the shots.

By the time I got up to go, bats were flittering between the stones and the last light of the afternoon was being soaked up by the river bend to Norham. Its frayed castle keep was silhouetted above the trees against a darkening sky. The raised fist of the cult of St Cuthbert. I walked back across the bridge into the part of England once known as St Cuthbert's Land. It was a political rather than a religious description, a cynical deployment of saintly memory designed to put the fear of God into the people, to make them realize on which side their bread was buttered and on which side of a disputed frontier their loyalties should lie.

CHAPTER FIFTEEN

Ruins of Norham Castle

I f I'd been walking along this riverside path to Norham one late afternoon in 1797, I might have had as a companion a rather down-at-heel retired naval officer called Admiral Booth. At least that's how he described himself if people were nosey. By all accounts he wouldn't have been much fun to be with. An acquaintance described him as morose, tasteless and slovenly. But he'd have been worth meeting for all that because he's better known as 'the great pyrotechnist' and 'the painter of light', even 'the first impressionist'.

Joseph Mallord William Turner painted Norham as a brutal memory in the mist. Luminous, atmospheric. History seen through a bold, swirling prism of colour. The paintings he completed from a sketch made on that visit to the Border capture for me the contradictory essence of life as it was on this frontier. Cattle stand untroubled in the water. There's a hint of movement along the river, perhaps a fisherman calmly casting his net for the salmon. What passed for normal daily life in the welcome pauses between battle and raid. But over it all there's the ghostly, half-ruined keep of Norham Castle. Through the gaps in its broken walls there whistles an asthmatic, sinister breath. Wraiths and frets that haunt what Henry VIII's chronicler, John Leland, described as 'the danngerest place in England'.

During the Anglo-Scottish wars Norham was threat and target in equal measure. Built by three of Durham's bishop princes it was started in 1121 and the mortar was scarcely dry before the Scots had it in bits.

Men from the wilds of Galloway, the Orkneys and Western Isles and the half-savage clans from the north have clamoured and howled around its walls spending their rage and strength. From the uttermost parts of Christendom warriors and knights, famed for their skill in arms, have journeyed hither to test the temper of their steel against a foe worthy of their skill and courage and, peradventure, won the applause and affections of many a faire lady. Such romantic deeds of chivalry stir the hearts of men with emotion and shed a lustre over the terrible realities of war, the bitter contentions of centuries and the base acts of designing Kings.[40]

It sounds like the trailer for Norham – the movie.

But I suspect Mr Bogg's concentration on the uplifting qualities of chivalry rather misses the point. Border warfare had little time for a dab of scent behind the faire lady's ear and was much, much more to do with the forced evacuation of bodily fluids. Blood, snot and excrement were Norham's stock in trade.

Chivalry did matter to a certain lofty class of Border fighters. Kings and their knightly hangers-on saw it as a direct link between them and the perfumed age of Arthurian glory. By adhering to its rituals they were reinforcing their right to be part of the mysterious succession. Honours, then as now, were a cheap way of buying loyalty and service. There were chivalrous moments in some of the nastiest of Border battles – doomed charges in the face of overwhelming odds, acts of selfless courage, the laying down of life for friend or figurehead. Individual courage was honoured. But for most Borderers the battleline was a butcher's shop.

But there was one great gathering here that may, just, have lived up to Edmund Bogg's vision of medieval splendour. It took place in early summer 1291, the year after the Treaty of Birgham had given Edward I what he had coveted for so long

40 Edmund Bogg, *A Thousand Miles of Wandering in the Border Country*, Mawson, Swan and Morgan, Newcastle, 1898

– a say in the Scottish succession. Scots and English barons sat as a court of inquiry with Edward as its president to decide who would be king of Scotland after the death of the Maid of Norway. Some say the court sat in Norham church. Others (and I prefer this version) that the assembly met on a bit of Scotland in the middle of the Tweed called Blount Island. It's a scruffy little grassy hummock, overshadowed by Norham Castle looming on its rocky outcrop. But that day it was turned into the Field of the Cloth of Gold. Crowds gathered on both sides of the river to watch the spectacle. Norham's battlements were thronged. More than sixty English barons were in attendance, together with St Cuthbert's army of monks in scarlet and green, led by the warrior Prince Bishop, Anthony Bek, wearing a pearl-encrusted mitre and carrying a jewelled staff. Trumpets echoed along the river as King Edward splashed his horse through the shallows and rode through the crowd to take his place on a throne raised in a brightly striped and open-sided tent. He wore a golden crown, a robe of scarlet silk and a tabard richly embroidered with the arms of England and France.

The various candidates for the Scottish Crown came before him to plead their case. By the end of the day there was a shortlist of two, Robert de Brus and John de Baliol. The rest, however good their references, had been given their expenses out of petty cash and sent home. Eventually Baliol would be handed the poisoned chalice as Edward's creature perched unsteadily on the Scottish throne, but the trouble springing from that was still a way off. This was an afternoon for heraldic fanfares and courtly gestures, feasting and fancy. The royal icing on a worm-eaten cake.

Sitting there dozing on the riverbank below Norham Castle, I was imagining that Technicolor version of Border history being played out on the island in front of me. If I'd had a flag emblazoned with the arms of England and France I'd have waved it as King Edward rode by on his way back to the castle. Because we're still suckers for it. Having been an outside broadcast commentator for the BBC for a lot of years, I know the boundless fascination aroused in the unemployed of Wolverhampton and the underprivileged of Deptford by the merest mention of a Lord Great Chamberlain or Rush Strewer of the Bedchamber. We proudly tell people that nobody does ceremonial better. Which means what, exactly? That nobody keeps a privileged elite in power by dressing them up in baloney better than we do?

Not that I'd like you to get the idea that I'm anti-royalist. The royal family, with all their faults, are better by far than certain presidents we could mention. It's just that we shouldn't pretend state ceremonial is anything more than an operatic version of music hall. Many of the great events of the state calendar are relatively recent inventions. Queen Victoria's advisors were dab hands at creating them to try to head off the groundswell of unpopularity that the grieving monarch's withdrawal from public life began to generate after the death of Prince Albert. The idea that events such as Trooping the Colour are part of a glorious British continuum that links Charles III to Edward I with an essence of Arthurian chivalry mixed in for good measure is an embroidered fiction. But that's no bad thing. The martial music, the dust of Horseguards Parade, the sun glinting on cuirass and helmet all generate a cosy contentment that politicians would be happy to make their researchers die for. It's all part of the process of stage management that's raised the curtain on every act of nation building since Nausithous the Magnificent was ruler of Albion. The Border was an important part of the stage on which kings, usurpers and chancers with delusions of grandeur strutted their stuff.

And as long as you can keep war and lawlessness in check it's all reasonably harmless fun. If the royal family wants to live in a suburb of Gormenghast, that's just fine by me. And wouldn't Titus Groan and Steerpike have cut a dash as reivers? And isn't it a shame that Mervyn Peake didn't write a deranged history of the Borders?

'Why would he need to when you already have?' I muttered darkly to the man waving the flag emblazoned with the arms of England on one side and Gormenghast on the other as I unfolded aching limbs, gave a final bow to the assembled company on the island and set off up the hill to Norham Castle.

When I got there it was shrouded in scaffolding, which really isn't good enough. They've had since 1513 to repair it, which I'd have thought was time enough for anybody. Even the builder who's converting my friend's holiday home in Tuscany would have had it finished by now.

The rotten cold came the next day. I knew I'd been sickening for something.

So with nose dripping I took a trudge round Norham village the next morning. I looked into Norham church (just in case the Longshanks meeting had happened there rather than on the island). The arcade of round Norman arches on the south side of the nave is spectacular and, according to the church leaflet, they're the widest Norman arches to be found in any parish church still in use. Quite why the Victorian restorers put incongruous octagonal arches on the north side of the nave is hard to fathom. But it's had a rough old time, St Cuthbert's Norham. Robert the Bruce attacked it and used it as a gun platform in 1320 when he was besieging the castle. For a hundred years after Flodden it stood roofless. It's also had a few unchristian soakings from the River Tweed. During a restoration in the 1880s almost two feet of river mud was removed from the floor, revealing pillar bases that nobody knew were there. It was probably stories about the flooding of Norham that persuaded James IV to build his Ladykirk on the hill across the river.

And Norham church is further evidence of the military and political role played by Cuthbert's followers. The present building was started in 1165 at the same time as the castle and probably designed by the same architect. There had been an earlier stone church on the site, built in 830 just two hundred years after St Aidan came through here on his way from Iona via Carlisle to establish the monastery at Lindisfarne. The combined reputations of Aidan and Cuthbert, whose body lay in the church for a while on the flight to Durham, gave Norham a particular power. St Ceolwulph, King of Northumbria, and Gospatrick, the 1st Earl of Northumberland, were both buried in the old church.

Norham's a dapper little village that doesn't show the slightest sign of being 'the danngerest place in England'. With its pub and its village green it could be in soft Hampshire. But even though it's best remembered for its part in Border warfare it also stood in the path of the Border raiders who filled in the gaps between battles by carrying their own fiery brand of mayhem along and across the Tweed. One notable incursion happened in 1597, which was a particularly bad year for Border bloodletting, and which introduces us to two Roberts who vividly illustrate the contradictions and complexities of frontier life in the sixteenth century.

Robert Kerr of Cessford was a thug. If there had been anti-social behaviour orders in the sixteenth century, he would have had the national ASBO collection. By the time he was twenty-five he'd been involved in four murders, and those are just the ones that made it into the Border records. But none of this juvenile delinquency held him back. He became a Privy Councillor and the 1st Duke of Roxburgh.

Robert Carey was a gentleman and probably the very nicest man to hold the office of March Warden. The account in his memoirs suggests he disliked having to hang reivers, but he enjoyed bold escapades in the saddle in pursuit of them. He devised a method of capturing pele towers by sending a squad of men on to the roof, lifting the stone slabs and dropping on to the huddled inhabitants. He was bold and brave and up for a challenge. He once won a £2,000 bet by walking from London to Berwick. He became the 1st Earl of Monmouth.

They both managed to live into their eighties and they both died peacefully in their beds.

The two Roberts started out as sworn enemies and ended firm friends. In the intervening years they led each other a merry dance. The 1597 trouble started because Carey managed to overcome his better nature and hang one of Robert Kerr's friends, a full-time reiver and part-time psychopath called Geordie Burn. Kerr wanted blood and revenge and came down on the Border like a wolf on the fold, as they say. He sent raiding parties into England in the hope of tempting Carey to come out and fight. The Warden was too canny for that and bided his time until news reached him that Kerr and his riders had been overheard at a football match in Kelso plotting a major raid south of Wark. Then as now, it seems, football attracted the wrong sort of people. Carey organized an ambush but just in time realized his spies had been set up. The real target was his tithe collectors, who were meeting that night at the pub in Norham. Carey got to them just in time, bundling them and their moneybags into the castle just before Robert Kerr and his 100 riders crashed through the door of the inn, drank themselves into a righteous frenzy of indignation, knocked the village about and rode unsteadily back into Scotland.

The following year, after prolonged and at times violent negotiation between the English and Scots authorities, Kerr was handed over to England to answer for his crimes. The man he chose as his jailer was Robert Carey. Apparently, rather like a scene from *The Odd Couple*, the two men bickered for four days. Without a doubt Robert Kerr was the one who left beer cans and dirty socks under his bed and it was Robert Carey who Hoovered during parties.

Something medicinal beckoned, so I snuffled into a corner of the pub, which was otherwise empty at that time of day. The weather was so gloomy, barely approaching daylight at grey noon, that the light from the pub window lit up the pavement outside. Maybe it was a particularly strong whisky mac but I could have sworn a mud-spattered rider galloped up the main street, captured for a fleeting moment in the spill of lamplight. It was the same Robert Carey, but this time spurring his way towards a grander supporting role in Border history.

In early 1603 Carey was in London. Queen Elizabeth was grievously ill. Carey's sister, Philadelphia, was one of the Queen's courtiers of the bedchamber. Some months earlier James VI of Scotland, with whom she'd had a long correspondence, had sent her a blue sapphire ring to give to Elizabeth with the instruction that Philadelphia should return it to him by special messenger as confirmation of the Queen's death and his accession to the English throne.

Whitehall Palace whispered with rumours of recoveries and relapses. The Queen was taking an unconscionably long time to die. Any number of courtly hangers-on wanted to be the one to carry the news to King James. Carey was determined to beat the lot of them. Set on putting himself firmly in the eye of the new King's favour, he arranged for post horses to be held for him the length of the Great North Road.

Shortly after one o'clock on the morning of Thursday 24 March the Queen passed away 'mildly like a lamb, easily like a ripe apple from the tree', in the words of her chaplain. She wouldn't name a successor to the very end. When pressed by her secretary, Robert Cecil, with almost her last breath she said quietly, 'Who should that be but our cousin of Scotland.' When he heard the news, Carey evaded his rivals in the maze of Whitehall's subterranean passages and rode out of the palace, stopping briefly beneath Philadelphia's window to gather up the blue ring she threw down to him (which some say had been cut from Elizabeth's swollen finger).

That night Carey was in Doncaster. On Friday he rode to his house at Widdrington in Northumberland, where he left instructions that James should be proclaimed King of England in Alnwick and Morpeth. He said that his officers should prepare themselves for the trouble on the Border that, as night follows day, would surely erupt when news of the Queen's death and nervousness about a new King became gossip on the streets.

By noon on the Saturday Carey was galloping through the pool of light outside my pub window in Norham, across the ford on the Tweed and into Scotland. Shortly afterwards his horse threw him and he was kicked in the head. For the last forty or fifty miles his progress was painfully slow, but by Saturday night he was clattering across the cobbled approach to Holyrood Palace in Edinburgh, having covered the best part of 400 hard miles in about 59 hours.

King James had gone to bed and Carey, muddy, bloodstained and smelling of sweat and horses, must have come as a rude awakening. But he had the blue ring in his pocket and when James saw it he knew he had the throne. What almost four hundred years of military adventure hadn't been able to achieve was accomplished in a candlelit moment between a King in a nightie and a Border Warden in mud, blood and tatters. As Carey bowed low and limped backwards to the bedchamber door and James looked out over the flickering lights of what had just become a less important capital city, already the old Border was coming to an end.

The man who would start to reshape it was, arguably, the most experienced monarch to accede to the English throne since William the Conqueror. He was thirty-seven and had ruled Scotland for the past eighteen years. He cast himself in the mould of the Christian Roman Emperor Constantine and aspired to create a Protestant empire of Great Britain. He believed he was the man destined to fulfil the Arthurian prophecy. There had been rumours in Edinburgh that if he won Elizabeth's throne he would change his name to Arthur. He also had widespread goodwill from an English population that had feared a contested succession and civil war.

When he addressed the first assembled Parliament of the reign in March 1604, he adapted the words of the marriage service as his text. 'What God hath conjoined let no man separate. I am the husband and all the whole isle is my lawful wife. I am the head and it is my body. I am the shepherd and it is my flock.'

In the first weeks of his reign the Border could have disappeared altogether. There were those who took the accession of James to the English throne as a cue for action. They argued that Scotland should be incorporated into England as Wales had already been. But incorporation would have involved conquest and there wasn't the stomach for it. James himself believed in a union of his kingdoms achieved peacefully and organically by winning hearts and minds, and in 1607 he warned his subjects to be patient.

It is no more unperfect, as now is projected, than a child that is born without a beard. It is now perfect in my title and descent, though it is not accomplisht and full union; for that Time hath all the lineaments and parts of a body, yet it is but an Embrio and no child; and shall be born, though it then be a perfect child yet it is no man; it must gather strength and perfection by Time.[41]

What James wanted was a perfect union. 'One King, one Flock, one Law', was the way he put it. And it seemed he was the man to deliver it. It's said he was the best-educated monarch ever to sit on an English or Scottish throne and certainly the only one with a working grasp of political philosophy. A recent profile of James concludes that 'He deserves to be remembered as "James the Just" or "James the Well-intentioned". Given the fact that the vast majority of rulers merit no such appellation, James's subjects were lucky to have him as their king.'[42]

Unfortunately his English subjects saw him as Scottish. He was rude and uncivil, forever fiddling with his codpiece while he dribbled and stumbled. He perhaps suffered from the royal disease porphyria, which later afflicted George III, or even from a mild form of cerebral palsy, but Scottish would do. His critics were quite happy to agree with Henri IV that he was 'the most learned fool in Christendom'.

In October 1604 he issued a decree proclaiming himself King of Great Britain, France and Ireland. The following month he created a common Anglo-Scottish currency, which had a twenty-shilling coin called a Unite. In 1606 he unfurled the union flag.

The Scots were keen supporters of the King James plan and tried, time and again through the seventeenth century, to push

41 *Journal of the House of Commons 1*, as reported in Steven G. Ellis and Sarah Barber, *Conquest and Union – Fashioning a British State 1485–1725*, Longman, 1995
42 Roger Lockyer, *James VI & I: Profiles in Power*, Longman, 1998

it forward. But the English had lost interest in troublesome Scotland and were quite happy to watch it wither as a vassal state. (Maybe the hungover historian of Kirk Yetholm hadn't been so far wrong after all.) And there were practical problems that prevented the Scots from wholeheartedly pursuing contacts with their new-found English allies. They still needed a travel pass for a journey to England and the cost of living in London was generally beyond the Scots purse.

James tried to encourage the Scottish nobility by giving them English titles and suggesting suitable English marriages. He would bring about a union of his kingdoms one union at a time. But the English aristocracy were less keen to marry off their daughters to the sons of the auld enemy. They saw no benefit in Scotland. It had given them all they wanted. A king. For almost a century what they saw as the wild and backward country north of the Border was shunned. And of course the English have never been desperately keen on foreigners of any description. As an illustration of just how slowly King James's plan to win hearts and minds progressed and how ingrained was English opposition to union with Scotland, this poem by a bravely anonymous writer was published in London as late as 1697, seventy-two years after his death.

> Scotch vermin, Irish Frogs, French locusts: all
> That swarm both at St James and Whitehall;
> Though now advanced to all trust, all command,
> All offices enjoy by sea and land,
> Shall, when this Sun is set, no more appear
> Within the confines of our hemisphere.[43]

43 Anon., 'The Metamorphosis', *State Poems*, 1697

The image of an inclusive England mad keen on expansion towards a Greater Britain is a long way from the truth. Even when the Anglo-Scottish Act of Union eventually became law in 1707, it ignored the House of Stuart's desire for uniformity. It was to be a diverse union that permitted Scotland to keep its own legal system based on Roman rather than English common law and left Presbyterianism rather than Anglicanism at the heart of its worship.

But we're getting ahead of ourselves. It's just a short wander from Norham to Horncliffe along the Tweed. Trees along the way are festooned ten feet above the ground with dead grass and twigs and the plastic flotsam of earlier floods. Undercut wire fences still attached to their posts hang in mid-air, the ground beneath them having been washed away. In places it looks like a disaster zone. In that week in 1603, as King James mulled over his plan for peaceful union, it was.

CHAPTER SIXTEEN

Paxton House

The news of James's accession spread fast to places like Horncliffe, and the villagers there braced themselves for what they knew was coming. There was a widely held belief that the death of a monarch brought with it the suspension of laws imposed in the royal name. And there were plenty of people along the Border just itching to take advantage of the interregnum. The resulting chaos became known as Ill Week and it rolled along the Border like the bursting of a dam. Scots riders struck deep into England and rode back loaded down with plunder. English Reivers were happy to reciprocate.

King James, already on his way to claim his new throne, despatched troops from Berwick to various places along the Border to put down the trouble. They were too few and too late. Horncliffe and Norham and hundreds of other villages were looted and nobody was entirely sure which side did the looting. A few riders ended up as crow food, dangling from gibbets at lonely crossroads, but it was token redress. If James needed any further evidence that his Middle Shires were out of control, he and his down-at-heel Scottish retinue found it in the burned-out Northumberland villages and smouldering farms they passed on their way south. By the time he got to London and entered the city under a series of decorated archways surmounted by the figure of Monarchia Britannica and through cheering crowds he'd already resolved to civilize the Border counties. He would abolish the Border Laws, scrap the system of March Wardens and disarm the riding families. Easier said than done, he knew from bitter experience, but now he felt sure he'd be able to achieve it because he, alone amongst English and Scottish kings, had the great advantage.

The riders whooping their way home from Ill Week knew it too. With both crowns balanced on the same head they could no longer play off one side against the other. They'd lost their trump card.

And James had the example of an earlier Scottish king who'd almost managed it. In the middle of the twelfth century David I of Scotland had dreamed of Scotannia rather than Britannia. Descended as he was through his mother's line from the royal house of Wessex, he felt he had a greater claim to the English throne than did the French usurper Stephen. And he already held most of the north of England with the support of many of the northern barons. They had far more contact with the Scots King than they had with the southern court. David regularly held court in Carlisle and Newcastle and he took trouble to sort out their grievances. In fact the people who felt most estranged from David's schemes were the landed families in the Scottish highlands who got no such benefits. The fact of the matter was that the lands of northern England were more accessible and easier for a Scottish king to govern than were his own lands north of the Great Glen.

David had ideas and vision. He created a sort of monetary union which kickstarted the economies of northern England and southern Scotland and dramatically increased royal revenues. Silver from mines on Alston Moor was the basis of the Scottish currency and in the late 1140s David struck a new standard royal coinage at mints in Roxburgh and Berwick, Perth and Aberdeen. Also at Carlisle, which became, in effect, the principal mint of the Scottish kingdom.

David realized, perceptively, that cross-Border land-ownership and marriage – his ability to offer land and hand in return for loyalty – was the most effective way of reinforcing the idea of a greater, more stable Scotland. It underpinned the state building that David had been engaged in at Stephen's expense. Most notably David granted extensive lands in south-west Scotland to a Yorkshire baron called Robert de Brus.

So far advanced was David's grand plan that Henry of Anjou, the future Henry II, on a visit to the Scottish court in Carlisle in 1149, agreed that if he came to the English throne he would leave David in control of the lands he held in the north of England. Assuming no further expansion, the Border would have ended up somewhere in what in Margaret Thatcher's day became known as the Peoples' Republic of South Yorkshire.

The plan foundered because of the death of two royal sons. David's heir, Henry of Scotland, died the year before his father. On David's death in 1153 the Scottish succession passed to Henry's eldest son, Malcolm IV, who was only twelve years old. But as significant was the death of King Stephen's son, Eustace, the same year. Weak and spoiled, had he survived, the anarchy of Stephen's reign would undoubtedly have continued and the Scots, even with the problems of a minority, would have had a field day. Instead Stephen was forced to agree a settlement with the future Henry II and his unchallenged succession dramatically changed the political balance between the two countries.

In 1603 James I and VI hoped to emulate King David's diplomatic skills and at the same time prayed he'd have stronger sons.

I quite hoped the rotten cold that had crept up while I wasn't looking wouldn't carry me off prematurely. The weather and the nose were both drizzling by this stage, which made the walk past the fields called Hangman's Land to Horncliffe, perched on its bluff by the river, and then on to the Union Bridge, less entertaining than it might otherwise have been – which isn't very. James Logan Mack obviously felt much the same about this stretch of the Border. He didn't give it a single mention in *The Border Line*, jumping from Norham to the

Bounds of Berwick. In fact after Norham he wraps up the whole of the rest of the journey in twelve or thirteen pages. After almost three hundred pages of meticulous detail he makes a dash for the sea. After six summers of research maybe he felt he'd done his bit. Either that or he just found the flatlands of the eastern Borders a bit tedious.

Something must have been troubling him – otherwise how could he have resisted telling us that the Union Bridge, built in 1820, is 432 feet long between the suspension points, 18 feet wide and 69 feet above water level? He would doubtless have known how much it weighed, too, which I don't. I do know it was the very first large-scale suspension bridge ever built in Britain and that it was designed by Sir Samuel Brown, a Royal Navy captain who'd invented a new sort of link for chain cables. He was five feet ten, weighed twelve stone and went on to design a bridge for the Stockton and Darlington Railway, which started to fall to bits when the first coal train ran over it, and the chain pier at Brighton. Thomas Telford used his invention when he built the Menai Bridge.

From the Union Bridge, which wallows in a rather disconcerting way when cars run across it (Samuel Brown, RN with his sea legs would have been entirely at home with the strange motion), the view downriver is dominated by Paxton House, which should be enough to raise the spirits of the most jaded snuffler. Rising out of the trees on a promontory above the Tweed, it's probably the finest eighteenth-century Palladian mansion in Britain and one of several grand houses built by the troublesome Home family after they'd gone straight.

Paxton has the sadness of unrequited love about it. It was commissioned by Patrick Home, who'd been sent away to study at the University of Leipzig. Like all university students, he went in search of the best party. The one he gatecrashed was rather grander that the average bash in the student union or the back bar of the Firkin and Faggot. On 25 August 1750 he turned up at a carnival at Frederick the Great's Charlottenburg Palace in Berlin, where the guests were dressed as Carthaginians, Persians, Romans or Greeks. He met and fell in love with Sophie de Brandt, lady in waiting to Queen Elizabeth Christina of Prussia. His next letter home asked not for the loan of a few quid to get him through to the end of term but for his mother to organize the building of a grand new house to which he could bring his bride. Unfortunately Sophie's parents didn't approve of the match – obviously the Home reputation had travelled as far as Prussia. The house was built but the marriage never took place. Patrick was left with just a pair of Sophie's white gloves, which have pride of place in the house to this day.

Paxton is a beautifully proportioned demonstration of how the hoodlums who ran the Borders at the time of the Union of the Crowns adapted to King James's reforms and continued to prosper. We already know that the Borderers were born survivors, and if they could survive generations of lawless chaos, a spot of civilization wasn't going to bother them overly much. They just adapted their skills to the worlds of business and politics and empire and found they fitted in very well.

Looking through the mizzling rain across the river to Paxton, I remembered a description of the depth of character that was bred on the Border, which allowed so many of its people to grasp the new opportunities offered by the United Kingdom and turn them to their own advantage.

The coarseness of strength combined with acuteness and inquisitiveness; that practical, inventive turn of mind, quick to find expedients; that masterful grasp of material things, lacking in the artistic but powerful to effect great ends; that restless, nervous energy; that dominant individualism, working for good and evil, and withal that buoyancy and exuberance that comes from freedom – these are the traits of the frontier, or traits called out elsewhere because of the existence of the frontier. For a moment, at the frontier, the bonds of custom are broken and unrestraint is triumphant.

That was part of a speech delivered in 1893 by a young professor of history at the University of Wisconsin called Frederick Jackson Turner. He could have been talking about the families of Liddesdale, but the frontier society he was describing was the American West, different in so many ways from the Borderlands we're travelling through but, because of its hazards and opportunities, encouraging the development of a similarly self-reliant population.

They had good teachers. An unusually large part of that population of pioneers could trace their origins to the England–Scotland Border, many of whom had arrived in the New World via Ireland. The first United States census in 1790 shows that the greatest concentration of Border surnames was in what became known as the backcountry, an area the size of western Europe that ran from south-west Pennsylvania to Kentucky and Tennessee. In some places in the early days Borderers made up more than half the population. William Penn's 'holy experiment' to create a godly, virtuous, exemplary society in the lands granted to him by Charles II needed muscle to make it work. The Borderers provided it. James Logan, Penn's Scotch-Irish Secretary, deliberately planted what he called the North Britons in the west of the colony, where they could act as a buffer between the Quakers in the east and the Indian tribes. The Borderers had found themselves a new debatable land with no established government or rule of law. Armstrongs and Grahams and a score of other Border surnames joined forces to ride against the Shawnee and

Cherokee, Choctaw and Chickasaw in some of the most brutal Indian wars in American history.

As settlement progressed the Border immigrants left their mark on the map of the new country. In the Appalachians one of the most common place names is Cumberland. Most states have a Cumberland County, the Cumberland Gap runs through the Appalachian Mountains, there's a town called Cumberland in Maryland and the Cumberland River in Tennessee. But more than that, they left their character in the people. There was a prayer in the backcountry which ran 'Lord, grant that I may always be right, for thou knowest I am hard to turn.'

Frederick Jackson Turner's thesis was that the challenge of the frontier made America great and he has adherents today who bemoan the loss of that turbulent pioneer spirit. They argue that many of the ills of the modern world – bureaucracy and over-regulation, an increasingly risk-averse society, the inability of many people to fend for themselves or even think for themselves and the worry blanket of religious fundamentalism – spring from the loss of the frontier dynamic. (They omit to mention that the gun-toting, anti-government militias on manoeuvres in America's backcountry backwoods espouse very similar beliefs.)

There's even one group of Turner-quoting campaigners on the internet who argue we're on a slippery slope to extinction if we don't find a new frontier to stretch us, a new border where an unshackled human society can flourish. Their suggestion is Mars. Maybe I should send them an e-mail reminding them that an Armstrong was the first man on the moon. Certainly the next probe to the red planet should carry posters warning whoever or whatever lives there that the cyber reivers are coming.

You'll be pleased to hear that shortly after Paxton the Border abandons the Tweed and heads north along the Bound Road of

Berwick upon Tweed. For the first mile the road has been abandoned to grass and encroaching hedges. But this ancient highway marks the perimeter of a war-torn city state. Carlisle is known as the Border city but the title should really go to Berwick. It changed hands between England and Scotland thirteen times between 1147 and 1482. On 24 August that year it was finally ceded to Edward IV of England, having been captured by Richard of Gloucester, the future Richard III. But Berwick was so strategically important that, even then, it was given a sort of independence. The town and its 'liberties', the buffer zone around it, were described as being 'of' the kingdom of England rather than 'in' it. This diplomatic halfway house meant it had to be given special mention in royal proclamations and that led, some four hundred years later, to one of the strangest quirks of Berwick's history. When Queen Victoria declared war on Russia in 1853 she did it in the name of 'Victoria, Queen of Great Britain, Ireland, Berwick Upon Tweed and the British Dominions beyond the sea'. Unfortunately, when the Treaty of Paris was signed in 1856, ending the Crimean War, by some oversight Berwick wasn't mentioned so, technically, the town stayed at war with Russia. To the immense relief of the communist bloc, a supplementary treaty was signed by the Mayor of Berwick and a Russian diplomat 110 years later. As the Mayor said to him at the time, 'You can tell the Russian people they can now sleep peacefully in their beds.'

The other quirk is Berwick Rangers. Over the years it's certainly been more successful as a quirk than as a football team. It's the only English team to play in the Scottish League, which has to say something about the Border, but I'm not sure what. And yet I've happy memories of Berwick Rangers. When I was a cub reporter at Border Television, they were the subject of my one bit of sports reporting. When I got the match report back to the studios the editor said he wasn't sure if I'd been to a football match or the ballet. I wasn't let loose on the terraces again and I've got Berwick Rangers to thank for that. So my impressions of football are standing on a heap of cinders in a rickety tin-roofed stand (bought second-hand from Bradford City's Valley Parade Ground, if I remember correctly – and why on earth would I remember that?) while Berwick fans told me about their greatest triumph. The day some decades earlier when they'd beaten Rangers 1–0 in the Scottish Cup. The day I was there they were stuffed by Alloa or Arbroath or some such by a margin that could have been a cricket score. I think.

Just up from the river the Bound Road passes Paxton Toll, at one time a customs post on the Scottish side of the Border. In its day it was a mini Gretna Green where irregular marriages would have been conducted, but there's no sign of a major tourism development or nostalgia supermarket here yet. The road has become a narrow lane marking out the boundary of the pale stretching three miles inland from Berwick that was designed as a demilitarized zone between the town and Scotland, enclosing sufficient agricultural land to feed the people of Berwick, in case of future trouble. The enclosed meadows were divided up among the Freemen, who were each charged sixpence for every acre of ground they held towards the cost of making a boundary ditch between England and Scotland.

The road we're walking still follows that line, four centuries old, that dips to Whiteadder Water and across the ford and up the escarpment beyond towards Edrington. Ever since 1609, when the boundary ditch was completed, the Mayor and Corporation of Berwick have been saddling up on a summer morning and riding the bounds, making sure that the boundary markers are in place and that the Scots are keeping their distance. It's a cross between a stately progress and a gymkhana these days but the crowds have probably always got as much enjoyment from the sight of a freeman or town councillor unexpectedly parting company with his saddle and ending up in the mire. Slapstick is immutable.

At the end of the riding they canter back into the town, back within the safety of the colossal sixteenth-century fortification system of walls and bastions that was the single most expensive construction project of Queen Elizabeth's reign. And that's how important Berwick was deemed to be. Elizabeth was notoriously mean. When asked for several hundreds of pounds to restore the crumbling castle at Norham, she agreed to spend £2 14s. 9d. At Berwick the fortifications cost her £129,000.

Berwick had been a commercial powerhouse as well as a political bargaining counter. In the thirteenth century the town was described as being 'So populous and of such commercial importance that it might rightly be called another Alexandria, whose riches were the sea and the water its walls.' The description was appropriate because it was the Scottish Alexander III who had encouraged wealthy Flemish merchants to settle in the town. They built the Red Hall, a factory in the manner of the trading outposts of the East India Company in Canton or Hong Kong. They traded in wool and silk and grain, and for a time Berwick outstripped London as a commercial port. The glory days ended in Easter week 1296, when Edward I, on his first expedition into Scotland and on his way to lifting the Stone of Scone, sacked the town. In three days of violence two-thirds of its 12,000 inhabitants were slaughtered. Edward rode over the corpses on his warhorse, Bayard, and urged his troops to greater excess, ordering them to make Berwick's mills turn with the flow of blood. The garrison of Berwick Castle could only watch as the people of the town were cut down and the Flemish merchants burned in their Red Hall. When the castle was eventually taken, its survivors were allowed to escape through these fields to take news of Edward's wrath into Scotland. Berwick had become an enduring symbol of English evil to the Scots. For many years 'Remember Berwick' was a Scottish battle cry.

The green lane that's been the Bound Road so far emerges into the modern world and pitted tarmac close by the ruin of Edrington Castle, built on a promontory above Whiteadder Water. All that's left of this Scottish castle, originally built to keep an eye on the comings and goings at Norham just along the river and eventually to spy on the Berwick liberties, is ten feet of masonry pressed into service as a byre wall. Most of the stone was carted away to face the town hall in Berwick. The lands around it were granted to an Anglo-Norman Baron called Robertus de Lavedre by the Scottish king Malcolm Canmore for his part in the defeat of Mac Bethad Mac Findleach at Birnam in 1054.

Students of the Scottish play may be interested to hear that just along the road from Edrington Castle is a place called Witches Cleuch, alive with newts and toads, where they were still burning women for sorcery in the late eighteenth century.

The Lavedre family name eventually became Lauder and a later owner of Edrington, Sir George Lauder, was a friend of James VI and tutor to his son, Prince Henry. One of Sir George's descendants was the first British entertainer ever to sell a million records, who was described by Winston Churchill as Scotland's greatest ever ambassador. And there are very few places that can get you from *Macbeth* to Harry Lauder in less than ten lines.

By the time he got to this point James Logan Mack was demob happy. Pointing out that the Border line runs up the middle of the road, which is therefore a joint charge on the counties of Berwickshire and Northumberland, he even allows himself a word of slang. 'Here one can drive in cart or car for a mile and more, and claim to have had a "hurl" in both countries at the same time.'

Maybe it was happy memories of boyhood that encouraged him to be so slapdash. He used to holiday with relatives at the nearby Edrington House. What he doesn't mention is that it's a very spooky road. In both hedgerows the trees seem to be dying. He is a bit rough on the old Free Church of Mordington on Kirk Hill, long an outpost of grim Presbyterianism ten feet from the Border. He suggests that as it's unlikely ever to be pressed into service again it might as well be pulled down and its materials put to some practical use. Its owners presumably never read *The Border Line* because they've left it standing and seem to have turned it into a garage. But I bet they wouldn't dare do an oil change on the Sabbath.

At the next crossroads they've pulled down another, more ancient, Mordington church. All that's left of this one is a well-tended graveyard and a rather ugly chunk of sawn-off wall. Again it's so close to the road and the line of the Border that, as they came out after services, the congregation would have spilled into England. The priest of the old church at Mordington at the time Edward I was sacking Berwick and butchering his parishioners was Bernard de Linton who, unsurprisingly, became a staunch supporter of Robert the Bruce. He was his chaplain during the years of rebellion and when Robert became king was rewarded with the jobs of Chancellor of Scotland and Abbot of Arbroath. It was Linton who wrote the Declaration of Arbroath in 1320.

The document, signed by eight earls and forty-five barons, begged Pope John XXII to intervene in the struggles between England and Scotland. As we already know, it brought no instant solution to Scotland's troubles but it was significant for two reasons that were more important than a quick fix. It declared the independence of the Scottish nation and the right to defend it. The national cause was set above feudal obligation. In effect it proclaimed Scotland the first nation state in Europe in the modern sense. And perhaps more important even than that, it set the will of the people above that of the King. A monarch who broke his sacred covenant with his subjects could be removed.

> ... if he should give up what he has begun, and agree to make us or our kingdom subject to the King of England or the English, we should exert ourselves at once to drive him out as our enemy and a subverter of his own rights and ours, and make some other man who was well able to defend us our King; for, as long as but a hundred of us remain alive, never will we on any conditions be brought under English rule. It is in truth not for glory, nor riches, nor honours that we are fighting, but for freedom – for that alone, which no honest man gives up but with life itself.[44]

For all its faults, and there were many of them in terms of the laughable rendering of history that Linton used to bolster his case, the declaration was a prescient and very modern document. There are echoes of it in the American Declaration of Independence.

Good job Linton was almost four hundred years dead by the time the relationship between England and Scotland was eventually rationalized by political union. And even so, what was left of him would have been burling dustily in his grave. Because to all intents and purposes Scotland was brought under English rule and a crippling English economic dominance as well. I must drop a line to the Glasgow history teacher to apologize for ever doubting his analysis.

44 Declaration of Arbroath, 6 April 1320

In the run-up to the Union of the Parliaments, Navigation Acts passed by the English Parliament ensured that trade with the colonies was to be carried out with England only, in English ships crewed by English seamen. The intention was to create an English rather than a British Empire. Failed harvests in Scotland in the closing years of the seventeenth century led to widespread hardship. English protectionism was blamed and Scots opinion turned against any further union. Many thousands of people, a substantial portion of them from the western Borders, got out to Ulster and America. But the Scots left at home were brought into line in March 1705 by the passing of the Alien Act, which demanded that they abandon any idea of a restored Stuart monarchy after the death of Queen Anne and adopt the Hanoverian succession by December of that year. If they didn't, all Scots in England would be classed as aliens and most Scottish trade with England would be stopped.

Relations between the two countries were so bad that when Commissioners from both countries assembled in London in April 1706 to discuss political union, their negotiations were by memoranda passed between their respective delegations. It was a bit like trade union negotiators meeting at ACAS in the 1980s.

But eventually, through a mixture of bullying, apathy, bribery and corruption, a deal was struck. Scotland would lose its Crown, its Parliament, 112 of its 157 constituencies, its coinage and control over its economy. Eventually it would also lose its Privy Council and the Scottish Secretary. Unsurprisingly, the English saw it as a great victory and to reinforce the point the guns of the Tower of London were fired in celebration.

So why did the Scottish Parliament vote so readily for its abolition and for such a one-sided deal? You won't be surprised to hear that one reason is the powerful support for union whipped up by two influential Borderers – James

Douglas and John Kerr. They both got dukedoms from a grateful British establishment for their trouble. James Douglas became Duke of Queensberry (a title now held through marriage by the Duke of Buccleuch) and John Kerr became Duke of Roxburgh. Small world, isn't it?

CHAPTER SEVENTEEN

The end of the journey: the tunnel emerges on the cliff

I t was then the shooting started.

I'd just got to the corner beyond Mordington old church and was standing with one foot on each bank of a tatty little ditch called the Bailies' Burn. The Border follows the line of it out on to the shoulder of Halidon Hill, which is best known for the battle in 1333 when the troops of Edward III faced a Scottish army advancing to relieve the town of Berwick. The English bowmen tried out a new technique on Halidon Hill, a formation called the harrow in which they formed a sawtooth line which allowed them to shoot to right and left as well as straight ahead. It was the formation that gave Edward his great victory over the French at Crécy thirteen years later.

But this wasn't bow-and-arrow stuff. This was definitely shooting. A straggle of men with guns was advancing down the hill towards me. On balance I thought I preferred the KEEP OUT signs.

Then I remembered a bit of advice I was given by a battle-hardened campaigner for ramblers' rights who once bored the arse off me for an hour going on a fortnight in a barn in Borrowdale, where we'd taken shelter during a Lakeland downpour. He'd apparently had many a run-in with landowners who put their shooting pleasures above what he considered to be the inalienable right of walkers to wander wherever and whenever they wished. 'Safest thing to do is dress up as a pheasant,' he reckoned. Unfortunately my policy of travelling light meant I'd completely forgotten to pack the pheasant outfit so, discretion being the better part of cowardice, I decided to avoid trespassing into their shooting gallery.

Instead I grumbled off up the road past the rather overdressed hamlet of Clappers and the entrance to Mordington House on a detour that would take me back to the Border a couple of miles further on. Addressing no hedge in particular I hoped the bloody racket the shooters were making would waken the ghost of Black Agnes. She's supposedly buried in the grounds of Mordington House and was just the girl to sort them out.

Lady Agnes Randolph, Countess of Moray, was some cookie. In January 1388 the lady with the startlingly black hair and penetrating, flashing eyes found herself besieged in her husband's clifftop castle at Dunbar by the English forces of the Earl of Salisbury. They bombarded the keep, knocking chunks off the battlements and fully expecting the little woman inside to have a fit of the vapours and surrender. Instead Agnes put on her prettiest frock, instructed her maids to wear their Sunday-best wenchery and paraded on the battlements, dusting off the damaged stones with white handkerchiefs. Salisbury tried to starve her out but local supporters supplied the castle from the sea. The following morning she sent out a fresh loaf and bottle of wine to the Earl with her compliments. After five months Salisbury gave up. It's said that as his troops marched away they sang:

She makes a stir in tower and trench,
That brawling, boisterous Scottish wench;
Came I early, came I late,
I found Agnes at the gate.

I decided there and then that Black Agnes would have been the perfect companion for this journey along the Border. What troubles could a man have with such a woman by his side? Captivated by her bravado, I waved my once-white hankie in e direction of the shooters. As I don't have the chutzpah of Black Agnes, they probably thought I was surrendering. But at least they stopped blasting away for a few minutes, presumably while they discussed the strange apparition that was waving to them from behind a high hedge.

The detour forced me into Scotland. Into an oddly old-fashioned agricultural landscape that, five and a half centuries after Agnes's 'up yours' gesture with a duster, was forcibly taken over by the state in the aftermath of another war. That was in 1919, when the Land Settlement (Scotland) Act allowed the Board of Agriculture to compulsorily purchase a big chunk of this corner of Berwickshire to create the Lamberton Colony Scheme. It was divided into twenty-six holdings, and their houses and sagging barns still dot the landscape. Families were given a patch of frontier territory to work in an attempt to make them self-sufficient through subsistence farming. In the black and white photographs of those early settlers the pioneering spirit shines through in the scrubbed and smiling faces of men and women working the hay and carting the turnips. The deserving poor, ill dressed, ill equipped, but there to stay. The pictures could have been of a harvest in Indian territory.

Lamberton today looks as if it's gone to sleep. Or maybe even died. Once, though, this community on the Border was an important meeting place for sport and its grim relative, politics. Where the land settlement holdings are scattered across Lamberton Moor was the site of what's claimed to be the first racecourse in Scotland. And just try to imagine what gatherings there must have been up here on a bleak hilltop with its wide views over the North Sea and not a stick of shelter to break the wind from the Arctic. The cheering on of horses stretching for the line must have carried to Berwick when the wind was in the right direction. Here would have been assembled lords and layabouts (some happily ensconced in both categories), English and Scots, foreign visitors from France or the Low Countries, men of God and men of war, drunks and dandys (some happily ensconced in both categories). In fact a bit like a race meeting at Hexham or Carlisle today. Differences of allegiance set aside for a while for the altogether more important business of horseflesh and the thrill of the bet.

In political terms too Lamberton, perched on the Border, became a place of international significance. It was known to people across Europe. It took its name from St Lambert of Maastricht, who was martyred in Liege in 709. It was a place that attracted diplomats and treatists and spies. It was an acknowledged place of safe passage between England and Scotland. In 1573 during the turmoil between supporters of Mary, Queen of Scots and the Regent of her son, the seven-year-old James VI, the Treaty of Lamberton allowed the English Army to besiege and take Edinburgh Castle as mercenaries of the Scottish government. And that's about as mixed up a bit of treaty writing as it's possible to imagine.

But Lamberton's greatest moment was in 1502, when a thirteen-year-old bride was handed over at Lamberton in a ceremony that paved the way for the Union of the Crowns. The previous year Margaret Tudor, daughter of Henry VII and older sister of the future Henry VIII, had been married by proxy in London to James IV of Scotland. The Earl of Bothwell had played the part of the King for the purposes of the ceremony. Pope Alexander VI had given his blessing to the marriage but advised that the young Princess stay in England for a year so that she was ready to bear children when she arrived in Scotland.

The church at Lamberton is a stunted ruin. It was abandoned as a parish church not long after the Union of the

Crowns and became the private burial ground of the Renton family. Its surroundings aren't much to write home about either. By the graveyard is the peeling community hall of the old Lamberton Colony, which would look more at home on some Hebridean island. And behind that, propped on breeze blocks, is a mobile home which will never be mobile again but which has picture windows giving unrestricted views of its assorted contents of joinery and plumbing scrap.

But it was to this unlikely spot in 1502 that a great procession came, turning off the rutted coaching road to the north and coming up the hill to where a group of Scottish Commissioners waited by the church in the sharp, cold wind. Even after three weeks of uncomfortable travelling the procession sparkled. The Royal Standard of the Queen of Scotland flew at its head. There were footmen in white and green Tudor livery. The litter in which Margaret sat behind closed curtains was a confection lined with blue velvet and hung with cloth of gold. It was carried by bearers uniformed in red and black. Behind the litter, and too uncomfortable for long-distance travel on broken roads, was the Queen's state coach, its seats covered in bearskin, its horses draped with black and crimson velvet. Behind that more servants and a martial escort, a groom leading the Queen's horse, on which was a saddle embroidered with scarlet roses.

The Scottish Commissioners kneeled to welcome their young Queen and in the church prayers were said to St Lambert and the Virgin Mary asking for a blessing on Queen Margaret and divine protection for the rest of her journey to Edinburgh and her coronation.

There's no record of her great-grandson, James VI of Scotland and I of England, visiting Lamberton church on his progress to London in 1603. But he passed close by and it's surely inconceivable that he wouldn't have popped in. One thing nobody could accuse James of lacking was a sense of history and destiny, and in the little church at Lamberton they crossed. That moment when the young Margaret travelled into Scotland set a seal on his claim to the English throne. If he didn't stop and say a prayer for the soul of his great-grannie he certainly should have done.

I strolled down from the church towards the rumble of the Great North Road, now of course poetically renamed the A1. Flanking the byway to the church is a pair of whale jawbones set in concrete as a pyorrhoeal monument to Berwick's days as a prosperous whaling port. It's said that when the whaling fleet – the Greenlanders as they were known – came home, the town could smell it twenty miles away. You could probably smell them up here on the hill at Lamberton. Like slave ships their stench arrived ashore several hours before they could be seen on the horizon, their cargo of blubber fermenting in its casks. But it was a pretty, valuable stench. Whale oil lit the mines and manufactories of the emerging industrial revolution. It lit the church and the withdrawing room. It was used in the manufacture of soap and cloth and fertilizer. Whalebone shaped English and Scots society in more exciting ways. The burghers of Berwick held perfumed hankies to their noses and counted their brass.

The Border crosses the A1 at what used to be Lamberton Toll until it was bulldozed as part of a road-widening scheme. The only structure there now is the caravan of MacArthur's Border Reivers Snack Bar – mercifully closed the day I passed through. But a little cluster of cottages was still standing at Lamberton Toll when Logan Mack was a boy. He remembered his father chatting to the toll keeper who guarded the gates across the post road from Newcastle to Edinburgh and charged ninepence for each pony and trap and a double fee if the traveller had the luxury of a carriage and pair. Like the toll keeper at Coldstream and the blacksmith at Gretna, his main income came from the marriage business.

But what had fascinated the young Logan Mack more than any of these things was Lamberton Toll's international pigsty. The Border ran through the middle of it so that 'its occupant sleeps in England and has his meals in the adjacent country'. It's a good job young James took up the law rather than farming because I suspect the occupant would have been more usefully female. But no matter, serious issues of nationality buzzed about the Lamberton sty. Just before the First World War the farmer from Lamberton bought a pig at Marshall Meadows, half a mile into England, and walked it home. The Berwickshire authorities, after lengthy deliberation, ruled the sty (but not its exercise yard) to be in Scotland and fined him £5 for importing a porcine specimen without a licence. Such are the great matters of state thrown up by the drawing of Border lines.

But the farmer got his own back. Between the site of Lamberton Toll and the east coast railway line a couple of fields away the Border is marked by a wall. Another dry stone frontier preserving some long-forgotten boundary dispute in two curious double right-angled turns. As Logan Mack reported in 1924:

Many years ago it was proposed to straighten the March at this place and so do away with the awkward corners which interfered, as they still do, with the cultivation of the ground on each side of the wall. Naturally it was proposed that the cost of carrying such an improvement into effect should be borne at the mutual expense of the conterminous proprietors, one of whom was reputed to keep a tight string around the neck of his purse.

A string that had got appreciably tighter ever since he was stung for a fiver in the case of the illegal immigrant pig. 'When his formal consent was requested the virtuous man skilfully evaded the situation by replying in these words, "God forbid that I should alter the boundary of my native land."' He wouldn't and it hasn't been. The curious wall of the pig keeper's revenge is still there and still enshrined on the Ordnance Survey maps.

A more troublesome opponent than a slighted pigman is the National Rail Authority, which now blocks our way. Stumbling across the east coast main line is not recommended, leaving aside the sheaf of by-laws you'd infringe by doing it. To reinforce the point the King's Cross to Edinburgh Waverley GNER express appears out of nowhere and thunders off along the headlands. There used to be a jolly guard or train manager or whatever they're called these days who would proudly announce the moment when the train crossed the Border. But as most passengers now seem to be in need of surgical intervention to separate them from their mobile phones he's probably given up the unequal struggle. The England Scotland sign is still there by the trackside.

So instead of dicing with death by express train I'm going to risk a brush with oblivion on the side of the A1, heading for a detour by way of the railway bridge at Marshall Meadows back to the clifftop Border line on the seaward side of the railway. And forget the high Cheviot, ignore Hell's Hole and the sinking bogs of Hobb's Flow, this is the most dangerous half mile of the whole trip. The A1 is the road for which road rage was invented. Flapping, curtainsided trucks bear down like the legions of the damned late for their appointment with the apocalypse. I made it (well, obviously I made it) but I was wet to the knees with road spray, would probably have benefited from oxygen to overcome the effects of the wagon fumes (oxygen cylinders are something else travelling light rules out) and a strong sedative would have been welcome in that i would probably have eased my compulsion to drag a passing wagon driver from his cab and quietly string him up on a hastily constructed Border gibbet.

No, it's just common sense. There ought to be more gibbets from which to dangle cavalier wagon drivers and boy racers along roads like the A1. It would be a much more direct (and may I suggest more effective) approach to road safety than sneaky speed cameras. I headed down the track into the caravan park at Marshall Meadows. There wasn't a pig salesman to be found for love nor money, so my other idea of buying a particularly ferocious Tamworth boar with tyre-ripping tusks and telling it to go home to Lamberton along the A1 foundered too.

Sixty feet above the sea (that's Logan Mack's estimate, but I'd have guessed it to be much higher) the detour joins the Berwickshire coastal path, which goes north nine or ten miles by way of Eyemouth to the harbour at St Abbs. But we're only going to be sampling about quarter of a mile of it, skirting ploughed fields on the lip of a wall of sea cliffs that drop sheer to a boulder-strewn shore. An earlier line of the railway disappears into a walled-up tunnel. It was moved further inland after a steam-hauled express jumped the tracks here and went over the cliff. The farmer at Marshall Meadows told me that at certain states of the tide you can still see the wheels of the locomotive wedged among the rocks on the shore, but my visit obviously didn't coincide with the right state of the tide.

From every ledge and crevice of the cliffs gulls launch themselves into gliding freedom, wheeling out across a choppy sea, shouting over their shoulders to mates clattering and chuntering somewhere under our feet. And in the far distance, just visible in the layer of atmospheric shush shimmering to the horizon, are the grey ghosts of the east-coast shipping trade.

To do the job right I have to get back to the railway so tha the Fat Controller will only have managed to stop us from doing twenty yards of the journey. On the way up the hill worked out that of the 105 miles from the mouth of Sark to the east coast we've missed less than five, but I won't be more specific than that in case one of the sniffier landowners is able to work out where we shouldn't have been. Having come al this way it would be galling to have to spend the next few weeks defending either a trespass case in the English courts or alternatively, a criminal damage action, based on the alleged destruction of a number of blades of grass in the Scottish jurisdiction where trespass doesn't exist.

The southbound train whistling across the Border into the Liberties of Berwick gave me a double blast of its horns as strode down beside the sagging Border wall to the place where I could look down into the sea. This is one of the saddes Border crossing points in the whole journey. Unmarked Unloved. The wall's fallen away to almost nothing, replaced for the last yard and a half before the cliff edge with splintered stile and a rat's nest of broken wire. I stood on th stile for a bit with one foot in each country looking out to sea In front of me the ground fell sharply away by way of a grass bank that would be a bobsleigh run to your maker's door i you were daft enough to attempt it. But there below me on th shore was the last stub of the Border wall running out to th point where the tide nibbles at its foundations.

You can see it, but getting to it is an altogether differen matter. For fear of your mortal remains becoming the subjec of inquiry in an English coroner's court or a Scottish sherif court depending on which side of the wall you're washed up I suggest you don't do it. But I was going to have a bash Logan Mack said there was a steep path down the cliff jus north of the Border, but either the sea's washed it away sinc

1924 or the author had more finely tuned mountain goat skills than me.

Plan B. The farmer I'd met at Marshall Meadows said there was a tunnel that would take me part of the way to the shore. Which is why you find me disappearing into a hole in the ground between two static caravans. The hole looks like mining subsidence, a deep slump filled with long grass and saplings. A path of sorts doubles back on itself through the undergrowth and fetches up by an iron grille hanging off its hinges, beyond which there's a distant speck of bright light in the blackness. The tunnel is steep and slippery, cut out of the sandstone. Just inside the grille it's a high, dark vault with beams set between the rock walls. Nobody's quite sure when it was cut but we know why. Originally a stream-powered hydraulic engine hauled wagons up a tramway through the tunnel carrying kelp from the shore to use as agricultural fertilizer. As I crabbed down the slope trying to get my eyes used to the darkness to be able to spot ruts on the tunnel floor, the ceiling got lower and the walls closer together. I dislodged a stone that rattled away down the hill before disappearing into silence. And then it was getting brighter and the dripping echo gave way to the screech of seabirds and I stepped out on to a ledge twenty or thirty feet above the shore. There was a little alcove carved out of the wall, like a high-backed chair in sandstone, where the operator of the tramway must have sat, and I squeezed into it and spent a quarter of an hour watching the comings and goings of the gulls. It's a spectacular place, a great arc of overhanging cliffs fiery red where the sun catches them interspersed with the deep black of caves and fissures. The whole scene set to the music of a rolling, breaking tide.

It seemed far enough out to attempt the scramble round the northern headland of Marshall Meadows Point, which should take me to the end of the Border wall, so I set about trying to get down the last few feet to what looked even from this distance like an obstacle course of huge boulders. Somebody had been kind enough to fix an old ship's mooring rope from the tunnel mouth to the beach, which helped, but I was still covered in sand and other assorted grots by the time I got down there.

And the boulders were worse close up, treacherous with slime and seaweed. It took me twenty minutes of careful footwork to get to the point (as you've persevered this far into the book you'll know it's often taken me longer), but by then there was a layer of tidal green down one side of me from when I slipped into a crack in the rocks. Judging by the state of the tide, I reckoned I had about an hour to get to the Border and back before I was either wading or swimming. That's of course assuming that I hadn't broken an ankle in the greasy clefts in the rocks and had to be ignominiously hauled out by air sea rescue helicopter. Splints, morphine and stretcher are yet another casualty of travelling light.

But there it was. A part-demolished stub of wall on a low ledge above the sea. In the league table of anti-climax it would be hard to beat. We've walked more than a hundred miles to see a slumped wall. Even Logan Mack, the introspective traveller, was more than usually underwhelmed. 'Having accomplished this feat, he may seat himself thereon, and for the time being claim the distinction of occupying the most northerly point of England, and having reached the eastern terminus of the Border Line.' And that's how his book ended. No fanfare. No drama. No conclusion.

I sat on the wall, dangling a leg into each country and watched the steady advance of the sea. The Border, snaking a hundred and some miles through the landscape behind me to the mud of Sark, still does all manner of little jobs. Like a pensioner trying to fill his days. It divides Euro electoral regions and unitary authorities, constituencies and counties, parishes and private land. But in old age it's just pottering compared with the hell raising it caused as a youngster.

It was the Union of the Parliaments that forced it into early retirement. As Daniel Defoe wrote at the time about Scotland, 'She was before considered as a nation, now she appears no more but as a province, or at best a dominion; she has not lost her name as a place; but as a state, she may be said to have lost it.'

And by the time she got her Parliament back we were all Europeans in a bit of the world that frowns on Borders, that's committed to tearing them down. There's any amount of political posturing (as there was in 1552 and 1705) about protecting the integrity of our Borders, stopping the incursion of aliens and criminals. But the leader of the Tory party has as much chance as the Lord Warden of the West March of stopping them getting from Newcastleton to Carlisle.

If the Border matters at all it's to the very people who most deny its existence, to whom it's never made a great deal of sense. The people who for generations have lived on the frontier and whose history and character have been moulded by the line that made them a living: the line they ignored.

At which point I noticed that the tide had almost covered the rocks at the headland. I ran for it, which wasn't easy over rocks now partly covered. The little book of anthropological essays about the essence of frontiers fell out of my pocket and floated away. Some good comes out of everything. I scrambled over the bigger boulders round the point and a wave soaked me to the underpants. If anybody had been watching they'd have thought I was barmy. And so did I.

INDEX